UNIVERSITY OF GLASGOW
PRESS

WILLIAM HUNTER
1718 – 1783

A Memoir

Plate I Sir Joshua Reynolds. William Hunter. Hunterian Art Gallery, University of Glasgow

WILLIAM HUNTER
1718 – 1783

A Memoir

by
Samuel Foart Simmons and John Hunter

Edited by
C.H. Brock

UNIVERSITY OF GLASGOW PRESS
1983

ISBN 0 85261. 172.2

Printed in Great Britain by
Thomson Litho Ltd, East Kilbride, Scotland

CONTENTS

ABBREVIATIONS

Countway Library:	Francis A. Countway Library of Medicine, Boston, Massachusetts.
Douglas Papers:	Hunterian Library, Glasgow University.
GU. Ms. Gen.:	Glasgow University Library, Manuscript Collection.
Hunter-Baillie Papers:	Hunter-Baillie Papers, Royal College of Surgeons of England.
Hunter Papers:	Hunterian Library, Glasgow University
Hunterian Manuscripts:	P. Henderson Aitken, *A catalogue of the manuscripts in the Library of the Hunterian Museum in the University of Glasgow* (Glasgow, 1908).
Peachey:	G.C. Peachey, *Memoir of William and John Hunter* (Plymouth, 1924).
P.R.O.:	Public Record Office, London.
Thomson:	John Thomson, *An account of the life, lectures and letters of William Cullen M.D.* (Edinburgh, vol. I. 1832; vol. II. 1859).

ILLUSTRATIONS

ACKNOWLEDGMENTS

I AM most grateful to Mrs. Margaret Rickman who first suggested to me that the manuscript notes in the Glasgow University Library copy of Samuel Foart Simmons's *Life and writings of Dr. William Hunter* were in the handwriting of John Hunter.

I offer my warmest thanks to the librarians and staff of a number of libraries where I have always received unfailing help and kindness. The great resources, both manuscript and of printed works, of the Royal College of Physicians of Edinburgh, the Royal College of Surgeons of England, and the Wellcome Institute of the History of Medicine have been invaluable. Libraries in the United States, such as the Houghton Library at Harvard, the American Philosophical Library, the Pennsylvania Historical Society and the College of Physicians in Philadelphia, have a wealth of Hunteriana and doubtless there is more to be discovered in other places. Some come from the papers of eighteenth-century Americans who studied anatomy in London with William Hunter, some from the autograph collections made by Americans at the turn of the nineteenth century. Richard J. Wolfe, Curator of Rare Books and Manuscripts in the Francis A. Countway Library of Medicine in Boston, brought to my notice materials that otherwise might have escaped me. In its set of twenty volumes of notes of William Cruickshank's lectures and ten volumes of notes of the joint lectures of William Cruickshank and Matthew Baillie, the library possesses some of the most important, as yet unexploited material relating to William Hunter. Cruickshank and Baillie give the only record of some of Hunter's medical researches and opinions, and Cruickshank did not hesitate to use Hunter's bodily ills to illustrate his lectures.

Jack Baldwin, Keeper of Special Collections in Glasgow University Library, and the staff of Special Collections, which include the Hunterian Library, have given me every possible help and made of my time working in the Hunterian Library a real pleasure.

Over the last seven years I have had sometimes amusing and always instructive discussions with Fred A. Mettler, Emeritus Professor of Anatomy in the College of Physicians and Surgeons at Columbia University, and Distinguished Professor of the Uniformed Services University School of Medicine. His interest in and understanding of both William and John Hunter as men and scientists have been for me a constant stimulus and source of enlightenment for which, with his generous hospitality, I tender my sincere thanks.

x

I have to thank Libraries and Institutions for permission to use material in their ownership or care:

Scottish Record Office, Edinburgh
Society of Antiquaries of Scotland
Drummonds Branch, Royal Bank of Scotland
Royal College of Physicians, Edinburgh
Royal College of Surgeons of England
Wellcome Library of the History of Medicine
American Philosophical Society, Philadelphia
Pennsylvania Historical Society, Philadelphia
College of Physicians of Philadelphia
Library Company of Philadelphia
Houghton Library, Harvard University
Francis A. Countway Library of Medicine, Boston
Burgerbibliothek, Bern, Switzerland.

And for permission to use pictures or prints in their possession:

Her Majesty the Queen
The Trustees of the British Museum
The Royal College of Physicians, London
The Royal Academy of Arts, London.

Archibald Duncan and Alfred Brown read the manuscript and suggested improvements in style and arrangement. Mrs. Lily Hawick deserves my thanks for typing and retyping it. Stylistic lapses and errors of fact or judgement are my own.

C.H. Brock

INTRODUCTION

THE Society of Collegiate Physicians, of which William Hunter was a member, was founded in 1767 by licentiates of the Royal College of Physicians in London, who, though medical graduates, were prevented from becoming Fellows of the College because their degrees were not from Oxford or Cambridge. Their first resolve was to meet and dine at the Crown and Anchor in the Strand four times a year. At their second meeting they resolved to promote the science of physic and thereby the honour of the profession.[1]

Whatever the expressed objects of the Society, its real aim was to force the College of Physicians to include graduates other than those of Oxford or Cambridge in their fellowship. Those other graduates who were licensed by the College to practise in London gained nothing in return for the annual payments that they had to make to the College.

When formal approaches to the College failed to achieve any result, members of the Society, including William Hunter, attempted to attend a meeting of the comitia of the College to claim the right to take part in College business. Finding the gates of the College locked against them, they broke them down and forced their way into the meeting which was instantly dissolved by the president, Sir William Brown.[2] Gaining nothing by such means, the Society resorted to legal action, financed by the members, to which William Hunter is said to have contributed £500.[3] Litigation dragged on till 1771. The judge rebuked both parties but on his advice the College amended its statutes and admitted four licentiates as Fellows. William Hunter was not one of them for 'no person practicing midwifery is to be admitted a Fellow, be his qualifications what they may'.[4] 'Sir John Pringle moved that the man-midwife to the person of the Queen should be excepted, but whether or not Dr. Hunter's sins were too many to be pardoned at present certain it is that the motion was rejected by a large majority.'[5] From then on the Society turned its attention to strictly medical matters.

When William Hunter died in London on 30 March, 1783, he had been first steward, then treasurer and finally, since the death of John Fothergill in 1781, president of the Society. It was decided, according to precedent, that 'a general account of the life, character and works of the late worthy president should be read to the Society at their next meeting by some of the members who might have the best opportunities of being acquainted with them'. At the meeting on 7 August Dr. Samuel Foart Simmons read them the eulogy 'which he had written and which he had obligingly offered to the Committee to undertake'.[6]

Though Simmons had obligingly offered to undertake the eulogy he can hardly have been the member who had the 'best opportunities of being acquainted' with Hunter. Born in 1750 at Sandwich in Kent, Simmons was educated at a seminary in France. He was never a pupil of Hunter but studied medicine at Edinburgh and at Leiden, taking his M.D. there in 1776. Afterwards he travelled on the Continent and returned to England in 1778 and established himself in London. On 20 January, 1779, Dr. John Fothergill mentioned Simmons's desire to become a member of the Society of Licentiate Physicians. He was elected at the April meeting and thereafter was a regular attender at meetings; in 1781 he was elected steward.

It was probably only at meetings of the Society, or of the Royal Society of which Simmons was elected a Fellow in 1779, that Simmons met Hunter, for otherwise their paths do not seem to have crossed. Some thirty years' difference in age and the fact that Hunter rarely, in his later years entertained, suggests that they were unlikely to have met socially. They did have a common interest in anatomy and Simmons may have asked Hunter's advice over the publication of the first volume of his *Anatomy of the human body,* 1780, but if he did this is not acknowledged. He presented a copy of the book to Hunter, though Hunter probably never read it; the pages of the copy in the Hunterian Library remain uncut. Four years' slight acquaintance with William Hunter hardly qualified Simmons to write on Hunter's life and character or even on his works.

Simmons had to approach Hunter's friends and relations to gather up the facts of his life. From the information he received he strung together an account 'rugged as a pineapple and much more shapeless'[7] though as Sir Charles Blagden commented to Sir Joseph Banks, 'Simmons – like a good biographer – brings forward the strong, and glosses over the weak parts of his character with no small art'. Blagden thought 'the best part....was a letter from Mrs. Hewson containing a most affectionate account of her husband who was a man of real genius'.[8] After delivery Simmons's eulogy was directed to be published.

On 14 December, 1964, Glasgow University bought a copy of Simmons's eulogy at an auction of books at Sotheby's where it was described as:

> Lot 297. An account of the Life and Writings of the late Dr. William Hunter 1783. First edition, the author's copy, interleaved with corrections in the text and very extensive additions on the inserted pages. Evidently for a second edition which was never printed.

The book was sent to the Sotheby auction by H.A. Feissenberg, previously a rare book dealer and afterwards an associate of Sotheby's. Unfortunately he no longer remembers how he acquired it.

A comparison of Simmons's handwriting (Plate II) with that of the notes (Plate III) proved that they were not by him. When the notes were considered against the hand of John Hunter, William's brother (Plate IV), there was no doubt that he was their author.

John, obviously dissatisfied with Simmons's production, amended and commented on the text. Such is generally believed to have been the animosity between the brothers after 1780 when they disputed who had first explained the anatomy of the human placenta that John, in his amendments, whether for publication or for his own amusement, might have been expected to take the opportunity to vent his spleen against William. Surprisingly they show little sign of rancour. Although, on occasion, he slips in a note of his own contribution to William's work, the general tenor of his remarks is laudatory. The passing years must have dulled his feelings of resentment.

Simmons was not Hunter's only eulogist. Both Condorcet[9] and Vicq D'Azyr[10] composed eulogies for the Académie Royale des Sciences and the Societé Royale de Medicine respectively. Though it is doubtful if either of them had ever met Hunter, Vicq D'Azyr certainly was in touch with those who had and they, though they respected his scientific achievements, found little to like in the man.

Hunter has never received the full biography that is deserved by his medical and scientific work, wide interests, collecting and association with the political and cultural leaders of his time. Much new material for such a work is now available.

The numerous sets of students' notes of his lectures over thirty years, and of Matthew Baillie's and William Cruickshank's lectures, together with Hunter's papers at Glasgow University, give information about a wide range of his medical work that remained unpublished and otherwise unrecorded. Glasgow University also possesses much material relating to his collections. Matthew Baillie, Hunter's nephew, who was left the use for thirty years, of all William Hunter's possessions, before they were transferred to Glasgow University, kept possession of Hunter's private correspondence. This is now available in the Hunter-Baillie Papers deposited at the Royal College of Surgeons of England in 1895 and 1925 and with the Hunterian Society in 1965. Published contemporary diaries and letters, where editors not infrequently identify Dr. Hunter as brother John, and private collections of papers to which the public have access, sometimes provide unexpected sidelights on William. His bank account with Drummond's Bank is a mine of information.

Some use already has been made of this material. In the nineteenth century the main contribution to knowledge of William Hunter came from the publication of his correspondence with William Cullen in John Thomson's *Life of William Cullen* of 1832. Some of his correspondence with coin collectors occurs in the introduction to Sir George Macdonald's *Greek coins in the Hunterian Collection* of 1899. R. Hingston Fox was the first to make some use of the Hunter-Baillie Papers in his short life of Hunter in 1901.[11] G.E. Peachey, in his *Memoir of William and John Hunter* in 1924, attempted to relate the activities of the two brothers to the medical attitudes of their day. He made a considerable contribution to William Hunter studies by recording references to him in contemporary newspapers. Yet he left large areas of William's life unmentioned. Both Professor John Young[12] and Jane Oppenheimer explored the relationship between Hunter and his non-medical contemporaries.[13]

In *The Story of William Hunter* (1967) Sir Charles Illingworth makes William tell his own story and touch on some aspects of his life not covered by other biographies. J.M. Duncan did much to vindicate Hunter's reputation as an embryologist.[14] John Teacher's catalogue of the Hunterian anatomical collection, with its extensive introduction, served as a reminder of Hunter's wide interests in both human and comparative anatomy and pathology.[15]

But Simmons's *Life of Dr. William Hunter* is still looked upon as an official biography. It was but an evening's talk and necessarily a very brief account.

John's additions of much hitherto unknown material adds immeasurably to its value. When one imagines how much more he could have added it is to be regretted that John confined his comments to Simmons's text.

Whether or not it was John's intention to publish this amended account, it remained unpublished. Its subsequent history is a mystery until it turned up in the Sotheby sale.

Note

John Hunter indicated by an asterisk in Simmons' printed text where the additions and, in a few cases, alterations should be inserted and his directions have been followed, the added material being printed in italics. Occasionally it has been necessary to add a linking word – in square brackets – to make the text run more smoothly; otherwise no alterations have been made. Words difficult to read are prefaced by (?). The footnotes are those of Simmons. The numbered references are editorial comment.

NOTES

1. Minute Book, Society of Collegiate Physicians, in the possession of the Royal College of Physicians, Edinburgh.
2. L.G. Stevenson, 'The Siege of Warwick Lane', *J. Hist. Med., 7* (1952) 105-21.
3. Sir George Clark, *A history of the Royal College of Physicians* (London, 1966) II, p.561.
4. Letter to William Cullen from John Fothergill, 15 October, 1771. Thomson, 2, p.657.
5. Letter to John Fothergill from William Watson, 16 September, 1771. Thomson, 2, p.659.
6. Minute Book, Society of Collegiate Physicians.
7. 'Our Great Ones of the Past: Men of the British School, No. VII. William Hunter, M.D., F.R.S.', *Medical Times and Gazette,* 18 (1859) 391-393.
8. Letter to Sir Joseph Banks from Sir Charles Blagden, 28 October, 1783. Banks Papers, Dawson Turner copies, 3, 152-155, British Museum of Natural History.
9. Marie-Jean Antoine Nicolas Caritat, Marquis de Condorcet, *Oeuvres Complètes* (Brunswick, 1804) Tome 2.
10. Vicq d'Azyr, 'Eloges Historiques' from *Oeuvres de Vicq d'Azyr* (Paris, 1805) Tome 2.
11. R. Hingston Fox, *William Hunter, anatomist, physician, obstetrician (1718–1783)* (London, 1901).
12. John Young, 'William Hunter' in *Record of the Ninth Jubilee of the University of Glasgow* (Glasgow, 1901), p. 97ff.
13. Jane M. Oppenheimer, *New Aspects of John and William Hunter* (New York, 1946);
    'A note on William Hunter and Tobias Smollett', *J. Hist. Med.,* 11 (1947) 481-486.
    'John and William Hunter and some contemporaries in literature and art', *Bull. Hist. Med.,* 23 (1949) 21-47.
14. J.M. Duncan, 'Notes on the mucous membrane of the body of the uterus, William and John Hunter', *Edinburgh Journal of Medicine,* 3 (1858) 688-697.
15. John H. Teacher, *Catalogue of the anatomical and pathological preparations of Dr. William Hunter* (Glasgow, 1900) 2 vols.

ADVERTISEMENT

When I engaged in the following Biographical Essay, at the request of the Society of Physicians, I was aware that without considerable assistance my account of Dr. Hunter would be very imperfect. — The information I wanted has been supplied by the kindness of different friends, to whom I embrace this opportunity of acknowledging my obligations.[1] — For much of the early part of Dr. Hunter's history I am indebted to Dr. Cullen.[2] Mr. Matthew Baillie[3] has favoured me with an account of Dr. Hunter's unpublished writings and with other materials. My thanks are due likewise to Dr. Pitcairn,[4] Dr. Bromfield,[5] Dr. Denman,[6] Mr. John Hunter, Mr. Henry Watson,[7] and Mr. Charles Combe,[8] of which I have availed myself in the course of the work.

NOTES

1. Letter from S.F. Simmons to William Cullen.
   (Cullen Papers 1779-1788. Royal College of Physicians, Edinburgh), 5 June,
   1783.

> I have undertaken to read an Eulogium in honour of your late
> excellent and illustrious friend Dr. Hunter at a Society of Physicians of
> which he was President after the death of Dr. Fothergill. It is to be
> delivered if possible at our next quarterly meeting which will be held on
> the 2^d or 3^d Wednesday in July. You have probably seen the account of
> him which has appeared in the Gentlemans Magazine and some other
> publications. Part of that account was furnished by me and part of it by
> Mr. Combe. As I am anxious to do justice to so distinguished a
> character I shall be extremely obliged to you for any anecdotes which
> you may be able to furnish me with. Even his brother does not know the
> exact date of the Doctor's birth. I could wish to know something of his
> family – you was one of his oldest and most intimate friends and on this
> ground it is that I venture to request your assistance.

2. Dr. William Cullen (1710-1790), with whom William Hunter had worked
   after leaving Glasgow University. Cullen himself had studied at Glasgow and
   Edinburgh Universities, and after having been in practice at Hamilton,
   moved to Glasgow where he lectured in Chemistry and Medicine, and in 1751
   became Professor of Medicine. In 1756 he removed to Edinburgh as
   Professor where he held the Chair of Chemistry, and, from 1766 that of the
   Theory of Physic.

3. Mr. Matthew Baillie (1761-1823), M.D., F.R.S., son of William Hunter's sister,
   Dorothea. He had attended Glasgow University where his father, James
   Baillie, was Professor of Divinity, and had been elected to a Snell exhibition at
   Balliol College, Oxford, in 1779; during the vacation he worked with his uncle
   in London. He became Physician Extraordinary to George III, a warm friend
   of the Royal Family and is commemorated in Westminster Abbey by a bust
   and inscription.

4. Dr. David Pitcairn (1749-1809), M.D., Corpus Christi College, Cambridge.
   Physician to St. Bartholomew's Hospital, 1780. Friend of William Hunter
   and one of his trustees.

5. Dr. [Robert] Bromfield, physician to the British Lying-In Hospital? There is
   no known connection between Dr. Bromfield and William Hunter. Or this
   may have been an error for Mr. William Bromfield (1712-1792), surgeon, who
   was responsible, with Martin Madan, for planning the Lock Hospital for
   venereal diseases, to which he became surgeon. He was also surgeon to St.
   George's Hospital and lectured on anatomy and surgery. He had been
   acquainted with William Hunter for many years.

6. Dr. Thomas Denman (1733-1815), M.D., Aberdeen 1764, Physician Accoucheur to the Middlesex Hospital, 1769-83. His daughter, Sophie, married Matthew Baillie. This is the only indication that Denman was sufficiently well acquainted with William Hunter as to be able to provide information about him.

7. Mr. Henry Watson, Reader in Anatomy and Surgeon to the Middlesex Hospital; an early pupil of William Hunter.

8. Mr. Charles Combe (1743-1817), M.D., F.R.S., F.S.A. Educated at Harrow; apothecary in London, 1768. A noted numismatist, he helped William Hunter with his coin collection and produced a catalogue of some of the Greek coins in the collection, *Nummorum veterum populorum et urbium.* One of William Hunter's trustees, he was given an M.D. by Glasgow University in 1784.

A N

A C C O U N T

OF THE

LIFE AND WRITINGS

OF THE LATE

WILLIAM HUNTER, M.D. F.R.S. and S.A.

MEMBER of the ROYAL COLLEGE of PHYSICIANS,
PHYSICIAN EXTRAORDINARY to the QUEEN,
Confulting PHYSICIAN to the BRITISH LYING-IN HOSPITAL,
AND
Profeffor of ANATOMY in the ROYAL ACADEMY of LONDON;
One of the FOREIGN ASSOCIATES of the ROYAL ACADEMY
OF SCIENCES, and of the ROYAL MEDICAL SOCIETY
at PARIS, &c.

Read, on the 6th of Auguft 1783,
At a General Meeting of the
SOCIETY of PHYSICIANS of LONDON,
Of which He was
P R E S I D E N T,
And publifhed at their Requeft.

B Y

SAMUEL FOART SIMMONS, M.D. F.R.S.

Member of the Royal College of Phyficians, London;
Honorary Fellow of the Royal College of Phyficians of
Lorraine; and one of the Foreign Affociates
of the Royal Medical Society at Paris.

L O N D O N:
Printed for the AUTHOR, by W. RICHARDSON,
And fold by J. JOHNSON, Nᵒ 72, St. Paul's Church-yard,
M DCC LXXXIII.

AN ACCOUNT
OF THE LIFE AND WRITINGS
OF THE LATE
WILLIAM HUNTER, M.D.

William Hunter was born on the 23rd of May 1718, at Kilbride in the county of Lanerk. He was the seventh of ten children* of John and Agnes Hunter, who resided on a small estate in that parish, called Long Calderwood, which had long been in the possession of his family. His great grandfather, by his father's side, was a younger son of Hunter of Hunterston, chief of the family of that name.

At the age of fourteen his father sent him to the College of Glasgow. In this seminary he passed five years *being rather of a grave turn of mind* he, by his prudent behaviour and diligence, acquired the esteem of the professors, and the reputation of being a good scholar.

His father had designed him for the church, but the idea of subscribing to articles of faith, was so repugnant to the liberal mode of thinking he had already adopted, that he felt an insuperable aversion to his theological pursuits. *The family being intimately acquainted with* Dr. Cullen, the present celebrated professor at Edinburgh, who was then just established in practice at Hamilton, under the patronage of the Duke of Hamilton.[1] Dr. Cullen's conversation soon determined him to lay aside all thoughts of the church,[2] and to devote himself to the profession of physic.

* These were John, Elizabeth, Andrew, Janet, James, Agnes, William, Dorothea, Isabella and John. Of the Sons, John the eldest, and Andrew died when young *lads at the Gramer School;* James, born in 1715, was a writer to the signet at Edinburgh, who, disliking the profession of law, came to London in 1743[3] with an intention to see his brother William. *He took a liking to the study of anatomy and pursued it for some time, but probably he had too lively an imagination to follow any science for a continuum. He was much esteemed by Dr. John Armstrong, who often declared that Jimmy Hunter was the finest gentleman he knew. At this time he and Dr. Smollet wrote a comedy, which he brought down to Scotland to have it acted at Edinburgh,[4] which was never done owing to his being taken at once with a considerable haemorrage from the Lung, which produced a consumption from which he died, aged 28 years.* John, the youngest, is the present celebrated anatomist — Of the daughters, Elizabeth *died young,* Agnes *lived to be a woman* and Isabella *when about 13 or 14 years of age.* Janet married Mr. Buchanan of Glasgow, and died in 1749; Dorothea, who is still living, married the late Rev. James Baillie, D.D. professor of divinity in the university of Glasgow, by whom she has a son, Matthew Baillie, of Balliol College, Oxford, B.A., *who is Dr. Hunter's successor in anatomy,* and two daughters.

His father's consent having been previously obtained, Mr. Hunter, in 1737, went to reside with Dr. Cullen. In the family of this excellent friend and preceptor he passed nearly three years, and these, as he has been often heard to acknowledge, were the happiest years of his life. It was then agreed, that he should go and prosecute his medical studies at Edinburgh and London, and afterwards return to settle at Hamilton, in partnership with Dr. Cullen.

Speaking to me of the manners and disposition of his friend at this period Dr. Cullen observed, that his conversation was remarkably lively and agreeable, and his whole conduct at the same time more strictly and stedily correct than that of any other young person he had ever known. The same chearfulness and the same regard for prudence accompanied him through life.

He set out for Edinburgh in November, 1740,[5] and continued there till the following spring, attending the lectures of the medical professors, and amongst others those of the late Dr. Alexander Monro, who many years afterwards in allusion to this circumstance stiled himself his "old master"[*].

Mr. Hunter arrived in London in the summer of 1741[6] and took up his residence at Mr. afterwards Dr. Smellie's, who was at that time an apothecary in Pall-mall. He brought with him a letter of recommendation to his countryman Dr. James Douglas, from Mr. Foulis, printer at Glasgow, who had been useful to the doctor in collecting for him different editions of Horace.[†] Dr. Douglas was then intent on a great anatomical work on the bones, which he did not live to complete, and was looking out for a young man of abilities and industry whom he might employ as a dissector. This induced him to pay particular attention to Mr. Hunter, and finding him acute and sensible, he desired him to make another visit. A second conversation confirmed the doctor in the good opinion he had formed of Mr. Hunter, and without any farther hesitation he invited him into his family to assist in his dissections, and to superintend the education of his son.

Mr. Hunter having communicated this offer to his father and Dr. Cullen, the latter readily and heartily gave his concurrence to it; but his father, who was very old and infirm, and expected his return with impatience, consented with reluctance to a scheme the success of which he thought precarious. By the favour of Dr. Hunter's executors, I have seen the letter he wrote on this occasion to his son. In this letter he says, "Nothing has proved a greater comfort than the hopes of seeing you here soon; but your letter has cast a very great damp upon us all. I think you have been in a very extraordinary manner obliged to Dr. Douglas, and whatever opinion I may have of his present offer, or however unwilling I may be to consent to it, still I must thankfully own it, as a particular instance of his kindness to you. I surely must soon expect to be beyond this side of time, considering my age and present indisposition, being for some days past confined to my bed with sickness and a severe fit of the gravel, and would be glad to have you near me for the little while I shall be in this world; though at the same time I

---

[*] [W. Hunter] Supplement to the Medical Commentaries, London, 1764. p.28.

[†] Dr. Douglas, with great industry and expense, in the course of a number of years, made a collection of all the editions of Horace which had been published from the year 1476 to the year 1739. Dr. Harwood, who mentions this circumstance in his View of the various editions of the Greek and Roman classics, observes, that this one author alone, thus multiplied, must have constituted a very considerable library. A very accurate detail of these different editions is prefixed to the first volume of Watson's Horace.[7]

should be sorry to hinder you from making your way in the world, the best way you can – I wish you to consider well what you do. – With Dr. Cullen you may be very comfortably settled, and make money, and if you miss this opportunity now, you cannot be sure of it at another time. – Dr. Douglas's kind offer is only for a time. He may die before you come home or are settled, and leave you without friends at a great enough uncertainty. I suppose now you know very well the difference between the expense of living at home and abroad, and that perhaps cloaths and pocket-money may cost you more than your whole expence at home would do. You know my willingness to assist you, but you know too, that already I have gone fully as far as my numerous family will allow of – You must now do something for yourself. – Consider all these things, and if you can persuade me that it is for your good, I will not be against it".[8]

This was the language of a plain sensible man, anxious for the welfare of his son; and although it failed to produce the effect he wished for, it probably served as an excitement to industry.

His father did not long survive the writing of this letter. It is dated at Long Calderwood, July 28, 1741, and he died on the 30th of October following, aged seventy-eight years.

Mr. Hunter having accepted Dr. Douglas's invitation was by his friendly assistance enabled to enter himself as a surgeon's pupil at Saint George's Hospital[9] under Mr. James Wilkie[10] and as a *perpetual* pupil under Dr. Frank Nichols, who at that time taught anatomy with considerable reputation. *The Drs. course consisted of about 30 Lectures having but one body for the course and often not even that, the parts being shown on very good preparations. From the Dr. he learned his methods of making preparations, which was then a secret and every Pupil on this footting only was instructed in this art but they were bound to secrecy. Dr. N. had but two injections a fine and a cours. The fine was the spirit varnish collourd and the cours was wax resin and turpentine which was his corroding injection. But how far he may have been assisted in money by Dr. Douglas is not now easily known, but I know he had money remitted by his mother from Scotland, who took management of the family upon her, for in [a letter] to his mother, acknowledging the receipt of money, he made use of an expression to the following purpose, "that he no sooner got money, but which was taken from him by a number of Ravens". This letter I well remember having heard read to the family, and which expression was often repeated in the family. Another circumstance of his having money from the family, was his being alowed to draw upon Mr. Hamilton his relation merchant at Glasgow for money, to enter at St. Georges Hospital. I still remember having heard the letter read.*

He likewise attended a course of lectures on experimental philosophy by Dr. Desaguliers. *(He might attend Dr. Desaguliers, but it is to be remembered that a University education in Scotland includes every part of education. Dr. Simson was then mathematical professor and Dr. Dick experimental Philosophy.)*

Of these means of improvement he did not fail to make proper use. He soon became expert in dissection, and Dr. Douglas was at the expense of having several of his preparations engraved. But before many months had elapsed, he had the misfortune to lose this excellent friend. Dr. Douglas died on the first of April, 1742, in his 67th year, leaving a widow* and two children.[11]

* Mrs. Douglas survived her husband till May 5, 1752, when she departed this life at the age of 63 years. Her daughter, Jane Martha Douglas, died in 1744, aged 28; her son James Douglas, who set out in life with the fairest prospect, ruined himself by his indiscretion, and

This event, the probability of which his father had pointed out to him, does not seem to have retarded his progress. Such a loss, and at so critical a period, would probably have destroyed the hopes of any man of less abilities or industry than he possessed. But he seems by this time to have had a consciousness of the superiority of his talents, and he who feels himself equal to great things will not easily be dismayed.

The death of Dr. Douglas made no change in his situation. He continued *for some time* to reside with the doctor's family, and to pursue his studies with the same diligence as before. *But soon after the Dr.'s death he went to Paris[13] and studied under the different teachers, dissected constantly, for dead bodies were hardly to be had in London, and went through the operations in Surgery which he often mentioned in his lectures.*[14]

In 1743 he communicated to the Royal Society an Essay on the Structure and Diseases of articulating Cartilages.† This ingenious paper, on a subject which till then had not been sufficiently investigated, affords a striking testimony of the rapid progress he had made in his anatomical inquiries.

After some fruitless attempts by macerating and boiling *the articulating* cartilages in different menstrua, he had fallen upon a method not only of bringing their fibrous texture to view, but of tracing the direction and arrangement of those fibres, *which was by braking(?) the cartilage which brought out its natural texture.* He found that when an articulating cartilage was well prepared, it felt soft, and yielded to the touch, but restores itself to its former equality of surface when the pressure was taken off. This surface, when viewed through a glass, appeared like a piece of velvet. Thus he compared the texture of a cartilage to the pile of velvet, its fibres rising up from the bone, as the silky threads of that rise from the woven cloth or basis. These perpindicular fibres he considered as forming the greatest part of the cartilagenous substance, but he was of opinion that there are likewise transverse fibres, which connect them and make the whole a solid body, though these last are not easily seen, because, being very tender, they are destroyed in preparing the cartilages. *It is necessary to remark here, that in his lectures when on the cartilages of the joints, he always had the candor to make strictures on that paper observing he had been deceived, when he thought he had injected the cartilages, for in pursuing the inquiry further, he found it was only the cartilage in which the bone was formed that was vascular. Dr. Alexr. Monro makes a very ungenerous reflection on this paper in his attack on Dr. H.,[15] for he there endeavours to turn this candor against Dr. H., a strong proof that Dr. M. must have seen Dr. H's lectures.*[16.]

As he had it in contemplation to teach Anatomy, his attention was directed principally to this object; and it deserves to be mentioned as an additional mark of his prudence, that he did not precipitately engage in this attempt, but passed several years in acquiring such a degree of knowledge and such a collection of preparations as might insure him success.[17]

---

died about the year 1755, aged 30 years. It has been injuriously reported of Dr. Hunter, that he suffered his friend's son to languish in poverty, without administering to his wants. The truth is, that Dr. Hunter, after lending him at different times a larger sum than he could conveniently spare, was obliged to abandon him to his imprudence. Mr. Douglas's notes of hand to the amount of about 100L are in the possession of Dr. Hunter's executors,[12] *which was a considerable sum for Dr. Hunter at that time.*

† Phil. Trans. vol. XLII [1743, p. 514-521].

Dr. Nichols, to whom he communicated his scheme, and who declined to give lectures about that time in favour of the late Dr. Lawrence, did not give him much encouragement to prosecute it. But at length an opportunity presented itself for the display of his abilities as a teacher.

A society of Navy surgeons had an apartment in Convent Garden, where they engaged the late Mr. Samuel Sharp to deliver a course of lectures on the operations of surgery. Mr. Sharp continued to repeat this course, till finding that it interfered too much with his other engagements, he declined the task in favour of Mr. Hunter, who gave the society so much satisfaction that they requested him to extend his plan to Anatomy, and at first he had the use of their room for his lectures. This happened in the winter of 1746.[18]

It may not be uninteresting to give a short sketch of the state of anatomy in London when Dr. H. began to teach, and which now will hardly be believed. There were several teachers at that time viz. Dr. Lawrence who taught Dr. Nichol's course, Messrs. Bromfield and Heweat [Hewitt] both of St. George's Hospital. Their whole course did not exceed much 30 Lectures, which included anatomy, Physiology and the operations in Surgery, in which course there was but one subject.* On the contrary Dr. Hunter's first course[19] consisted of between 60 and 70 Lectures, into which he introduced six subjects, viz. one for the muscles and male parts, one for the viscera, Brain and spinal marrow with the female parts, one for the blood vessels, one for the nerves, one for the Peculiarities of the Foetus, and one for the operations in surgery, in which he shewed the art of embarming, at which time he proposed the method he afterwards put in practice upon the wife of Mr. Van Butchell[20] which method Dr. Black practiced or recommended (we may suppose) as his own because he says nothing of Dr. Hunter's having done it.

The no. of Pupils seem'd to correspond with the lectures of the different teachers. For the most the other teachers had about 30 each course, but Dr. Hunter had about 60 the first course and they increased as his course lengthened which became a course of above 100 lectures.[21]

He reduced the pompous oratorial mode of Lecturing to the simple and familiar discription, which probably on [no] man could excell. He was the first in great Britain that taught publickly dissections; for prior to this time, no pupil could get a subject, but what he could procure of himself, and when he ventured to get one, there was no one to instruct him. His improved course, the dissections of dead bodies naturally drew the Pupills to him.

The improvements in the practical part of anatomy were not less usefull. The shape of the dissecting Knif; the use of the Knif for then they dissected with scissors. The present dissecting(?) forceps; as also the length of the injecting pipe for formerly they were about three inches long as he was very anxious to prepare the diff. parts of the body, especially the vascular he of course improved the mode of injecting as also increased the number of injections for liquid(?) that he had learn'd from Dr. Nicols. He was the first that publickally in Lectures reprobated the vicious(?) practice of performing an operation quickly, and ridiculed the practice of the young gentlemen taking out their watchs to observe how long the operation was in being performed, which is now exploded.

He was not deficient in the discover[y] of parts and properties in anatomy. When a pupil in St. Georges Hospital he discovered the callus of Bones to be vascular and taught it at his Lectures, which was published many years after by a pupil of Dr. Haller. He discovered that the two first grinders shed which was many years after published by Albinus. He early discovered the beginning of ossification in the cartilage of the patella afterwards published by Dr. Haller.

---

* vide his Introductory Lecture [John Hunter's foot note].

The opinion of (what were called) Lymphatics being absorbents he has given the history of. All these were discover'd before the year 1748.

He was the only one that stem'd the course of our young Gentlemen going to Holand and France for their medical education, he even inverted the stream, and it is to him we owe the present state of anatomy, and of course everything that hangs upon it. He may be said to be the Father of anatomy in this Kingdom and indeed in some degree over the whole world for his course is the present plan of Lectures that is universally taught.

He was the first who oposed Hallers opinion of the cellular membrane being inorganic and shew'd that even the adhesions were vascular.

He is said to have experienced much solicitude when he began to speak in public, but the applause he met with soon inspired him with courage; and by degrees he became so fond of teaching, that for many years before his death he was never happier than when employed in delivering a lecture. *However he never got over a degree of anxiety in delivering his first or introductory lecture.*

The profits of his first two courses were considerable,* but by contributing to the wants of different friends, he found himself at the return of the next season obliged to defer his lectures for a fortnight, merely because he had not money enough to defray the necessary expence of advertisements.[23] This circumstance, which he himself mentioned to me, taught him to be more reserved in this respect, particularly as he found that by thus distressing himself, he had only encouraged the idleness of his companions. As he had always an aversion to borrowing, he now determined to be cautious of lending money,[24] and by adhering to this prudent rule, and strict oeconomy, he was afterwards enabled to amass that great fortune of which he made so liberal a use.

In 1747† he was admitted a member of the Corporation of Surgeons, *and in the year 1748 he invited his brother John to London, which was readily accepted. He came to London in Sept. 1748 just before Dr. H. began his autumn course; and his brother not disliking anatomy he was continued in it.* In the Spring of the following year‡ [1748] soon after the close of his lectures he set out in company with his pupil, Mr. James Douglas,[25] on a tour through Holland to Paris. *This was with a view to see what improvements had been made since he had been there before.*

Of this excursion to the Continent I have no anecdotes to relate, except that at Leyden he paid his respects to the celebrated Albinus, who amongst other things shewed him a preparation of the membrane pupillaris, and those admirable injections, as he afterwards told Dr. Cullen, inspired him with a strong emulation

---

* My friend Mr. Watson,[22] F.R.S. who was one of Mr. Hunter's earliest pupils, has told me that he accompanied him home after his introductory lecture. Mr. Hunter, who had received about seventy guineas from his pupils, and had got the money in a bag under his cloak, observed to Mr. Watson that it was a larger sum than he had ever been master of before. — Dr. Pulteney, in his life of Linnaeus, has not thought it superfluous to record the slender beginning from which that great naturalist rose to ease and affluence in Life. *"Exivi patria triginti sex nummis aureis dives"* are Linnaeus's own words. Annecdotes of this sort deserve to be recorded as an encouragement to young men who with great merit posses but little advantages of fortune.

†August 6.

‡I had some difficulty in ascertaining the date of this tour to the Continent, till Dr. Pitcairn recollected that Mr. Hunter brought him a copy of the *Codex Medicamentarius,* which was published at Paris just as he was setting out on his return home. The date of this work, which appeared in 1748, fixes the time of the excursion in question to that year.

to excel in that elegant and curious part of anatomy [Albinus also shewed] *his other preparations; but he thought that Albinus's preparations were to small or too little of the part; however he own'd it gave a neatness to the preparation; as also render'd the liquid cleaner, than when there is a larger mass. Dr. H. had at this time a pretty considerable collection of preparations,*[26] *many of which Albinus did not know how to make, such as rendering bones transparent and the corroded preparations, which methods he communicated to him but was much hurt by Albinus mode of rec[e]iving the information.*

His lectures suffered no interruption by this journey, as he returned to England soon enough to prepare for his winter course, which began about the usual time.

At first he practiced both surgery and midwifery, but to the former of these he had always an aversion *because he hated operations, would often faint at an operation, even disliked to bleed, although he studied how the art might be improved. He recommended when scalping, first only to make one incision, and if a fracture was found to follow it where ever it went, if possible, but by incission only, and then to act according to circumstances, for if no fracture was discover'd then the parts might be made to heal by the first intention. He was, I believe, the first that explained that the extent of the fracture of the inner table was larger than that of the external, and gave directions accordingly.*

He was I believe the first that explained, that the fracture of the Patella took place from the exertions of its muscles when the knee was in a bent state so that it brok as if over a fix'd point.[26]

He exploded the idea of there being air between the Lungs and Plura. Dr. Hoadly[27] *wrote upon respiration and endeavoured to shew the necessity of air being in the cavity of the chest. Dr. Hinckly*[28] *wrote a thesis at Cambridge in contradiction to this Theory, and J[ohn] H[unter] made the experiments for him in Cov[ent] Garden about the year 1752 or 3.*

His patron, Dr. James Douglas, had acquired considerable reputation in midwifery, and this probably induced Mr. Hunter to direct his views chiefly to the same line of practice. His being elected one of the surgeon-men-midwives first* to the Middlesex and soon afterwards† to the British Lying-in Hospital, assisted in bringing him forward in this branch of his profession in which he was recommended by several of the most eminent surgeons of that time, who respected his anatomical talents and wished to encourage him.

The Surgeons who were then in great practice were Ranby,[29] *Middleton,*[30] *Hawkins*[31] *and Bromfield.*[32] *Perhaps the history of the connection of the three first of those gentlemen with Dr. Hunter is as curious a part as any; it shews that men are always men, in what ever line, or in whatever situation they are placed. It exposes the little cunning friendship that is promoted by fear and interest. Dr. H.'s abilities upon which stood his character as an anatomist, which leads directly to surgery, became the object of jealousey with the three first, and revenge for being out done, was the leading feature in the conduct of the last, but it is believed the C-[Ceasar] H-[Hawkins] took the lead. The moment Dr. H. took pretty seriously to midwifery, he was in that line supported by the three above gentlemen, and I was often told by Lady — — — — — that Ranby used to say they were glad Dr. H. took to midwifery, for they were afraid of him, and their Hearts were set at ease when he commenced Physician, which neither interfered with the Dr. nor the Surgeons but we cannot say so much respecting the man midwives of the day.*

When in the Lying-in Hospital he endeavour'd to improve Midwifery. He allowed the women to deliver themselves, or at least give nature leave to exert her own powers. He even

* 1748.
† 1749.

alowed the uterus to dispose of its Placenta; all of which gave a new turn to midwifery; and instruments which had been to much used, were by Dr. H. almost laid aside. He also allowed milk breasts to take their own way, only applying poultices to them. He never opened or ordered to be opened any exumoses on a new born child's Head, which was often done by others.

But these were not the only circumstances that contributed to his success. He owed much to his abilities, and much to his person and manner, which eminently qualified him for the practice of midwifery, and soon gave him a decided superiority over his countryman Dr. Smellie, who, to the weight of great experience, united the reputation he had justly acquired by his lectures and writings: but his person is said to have been *large and clumsy*[33] and his manner awkward and unpleasing, so that he never rose into any great estimation amongst persons of rank.

The most lucrative part of the practice of midwifery was at that time in the hands of Sir Richard Manningham and Dr. Sandys.* The former of these died and the latter retired into the country a few years after Mr. Hunter began to be known in midwifery. [It was Dr. Sandys] *from whom he took the principle practice, which produced first a shyness in Dr. Sandys and at last he became Dr. Hunter's enemy and by ways of revenge he took to Dr. Bromfield as an anatomist and made him a present of his preparations.* I have been the more particular in tracing these circumstances, as the fortunes of his life seem to have turned chiefly on his success at this period.

As his business in midwifery increased especially among the people of fashion, he found it necessary to fix his fee for attendance upon a labour at ten guineas; but at the same time informed those whom he had attended before for less that he would still attend them at the former fee;[34] *for it may be observed of Dr. H. that his attachment to money arose from prudence not from a love of it, or a love to be rich; for whatever he was really attached to he was in the strictest sense a miser.*

Although by these incidents he was established in the practice of midwifery, it is well known that in proportion as his reputation increased, his opinion was eagerly sought after in all cases where any light concerning the seat or nature of the disease could be expected from an intimate knowledge of anatomy.

Having now lectured in the appartments of the Navy Surgeons till the year [17]50 he now wanted a House of his own to live in and took one in the same place (Covent Garden)[35] *under the Piazza, which was fitted up by the autumn course of 50, in which home his brother lived with him till the year 55, when he went to Jermyn Street, leaving his brother in Covent Garden to carry on the dissections and other anatomical pursuits, continuing to give his lectures there till the year 61.*[36]

In 1750 he seems to have entirely relinquished his view in Surgery, as in that year he obtained the degree of Doctor of Physic† from the University of Glasgow,

---

* Francis Sandys, M.D. for some time professor of anatomy at Cambridge, [37] was a most assiduous and able anatomist and had a large collection of anatomical preparations. He had all the parts of the eye finely prepared and preserved, and elegantly expressed in drawings. He was also very curious in his injections, and discovered the art of making them pellucid with oil of turpentine. Dr. Hunter, in his Medical Commentaries, mentions him as the discoverer of the *membrana pupillaris.* He died in 1771 in a retired situation in Bedfordshire at a very advanced age. His collection was first in the possession of Mr. Bromfeild and afterwards sold for 200 l. to Dr. Hunter.

†The diploma is dated Oct. 24, 1750.

and began to practice as a physician. About this time he quitted the family of Mrs. Douglas and went to reside in Jermyn Street.

In the summer of 1751[38] he revisited his native country, for which he always retained a cordial affection. His mother* was still living at Long Calderwood, which was now become his property by the death of his brother James. Dr. Cullen, for whom he always entertained a sincere regard, who was then established in Glasgow† *as professor of [Medicine] in that university,* and had acquired considerable reputation both as a practitioner and teacher of physic; so that the two friends had the pleasure of being able to congratulate each other on their mutual prosperity.

During this visit he shewed his attachment to his little paternal inheritance, by giving many instructions for repairing and improving it, and for purchasing any adjoining lands that might be offered for sale.[39] As he and Dr. Cullen were riding one day in a low part of the country, the latter pointing out to him Long Calderwood at a considerable distance, remarked how conspicuous it appeared. "Well" – said he with some degree of energy – "if I live I shall make it still more conspicuous."

After this journey to Scotland, to which he devoted only a few weeks, he was never absent from London, unless his professional engagements, as sometimes happened, required his attendance at a distance from the capital.

About this time he read lectures in anatomy to the incorporated Society of Painters, at their Rooms in St. Martins Lane, upon a subject executed at Tyburn. His brother who had the management of the Dissections had eight men at once from Tyburn in the month of April. This society were acquainted with it and they were desired to come and chuse the best subject for such purpose. When they had fixid upon one he was immediately sent to their appartments. As all this was done in a few hours after death, and as they had not become stif Dr. Hunter conceived he might be first put into an atitude and alow'd to stifen in it which was done, and when he became stif we all set to work, and by next morning we had the external muscles all well exposed ready for making a mold from him, the cast of which is now in the Royal Academy.[40]
[Plate V]

In 1755, on the resignation of Dr. Layard, one of the physicians of the British Lying-in Hospital, we find the governors of that institution voting their "thanks to Dr. Hunter for the services he had done the hospital, and for his continuing in

*Mrs Hunter died Nov 3, 1751, aged 66.

†In an erroneous account of Dr. Hunter which has appeared in different prints, we are told that about the time of his coming to London, Dr. Cullen, through the interests of a nobleman of high rank, was appointed to a Professorship in the University of Glasgow. But this is not true. Dr. Cullen remained at Hamilton till the year 1743, that is, two years after his friend had quitted it. The Duke of Hamilton, under whose patronage he had settled there, died in that year, leaving a successor, under age, and of course not likely soon to establish a family at Hamilton. This induced Dr. Cullen to remove to Glasgow. In the year 1744, at the desire of the University, and with the consent of the then Professor of Physic, he began to read on the Institutions and Practice of Physic, and a few years afterwards the professor resigned his chair to him. But in this matter no nobleman had any share. He owed his success solely to his own abilities and exertions. It is true, however, that while he was professor at Glasgow, and employed in teaching chemistry, he had the honour of becoming known to the late Archibald, Duke of Argyle, and by his Grace's patronage he procured, in the year 1755, a Professorship in the University of Edinburgh. The mistake seems to have originated in this circumstance.

it as one of the physicians"* so that he seems to have been established in this office without the usual form of an election. *He now relinquished the practice of Surgery, having obtained the degree of Dr. in Physic from the University of Glasgow (probably when he was there)*[41] *as a testimony of their regard, having educated him.*

The year following† he was admitted a licentiate of the Royal College of Physicians *but he never formerly separated himself from the Surgeons company, according to the by-laws, both of the Surgeons and college of Physicians, therefore continued in the list of surgeons, paid the annual fees and attended their dinners.*[42] Soon afterwards he was elected a Member of the Medical Society.[43] His history of an Aneurism of the Aorta appears in the first volume of their observations and inquiries published in 1757. Of this and his other essays in the different volumes of that collection, I shall here give some account, that it may be seen how much he contributed to its utility.

In the first volume, to the history of an aneurism just now mentioned, he has added some remarks on aneurisms in general. With a view to settle the disputes concerning the nature of diseases of this sort, he proposes a division of them into three kinds rather than into two, as had been commonly done by preceding writers. Thus, he observes, that aneurisms are either *true, false* or *mixed.* The first of these species he ascribes to a dilatation, and the second to a rupture of the arterial coats; the third, he thinks, is brought on by both these causes united. – He proves from his own observations in five cases, that such a disease as the *true* aneurism may exist. This proposition, though generally allowed, had been denied by some authors, who had imagined that in every aneurism the arterial coats are not simply dilated but ruptured. *In this paper, he makes some observations on Paul: Eg which are not commonly understood or admitted by the writers on the history of Physick; in which he seems to have laid a trap for the critics and which took for Mr. Douglas the anatomist, wrote a critisim upon that paper in the monthly review in which he censured Dr. H. for his ignorance of this author.*[44]

In the course of these remarks Dr. Hunter first mentioned a particular species of aneurism, of which he afterwards‡ treated more at large.[45] This disease, which till his account of it appeared had been totally overlooked, occurs when an artery has been opened through a vein, and a communication is afterwards kept up between the two vessels. At the suggestion of Dr. Cleghorn§ it has since been distinguished by the name of *aneurismal varix.* As it soon comes to nearly a permanent state, it is of importance to be able to distinguish it from the common spurious aneurism, as the latter requires chirurgical assistance, while the aneurismal varix, if left to itself, is productive of no ill consequence. A knowledge of this disease must therefore be considered as a useful acquisition to surgery.

In the second volume we find several papers by Dr. Hunter. The first relates to an instance of emphysema, in which relief was obtained by scarifications.[46] This case served to confirm the utility of a practice, which had been recommended by

---

* Extracted from the minutes of the Weekly Committee of the Hospital, dated June 20, 1755.
† Sept. 30, 1756.
‡Medical Observations and Inquiries, vol. II and IV.
§Ibid vol. III, [George Cleghorn, 'The case of an aneurysmal varix related and described, in two letters ... to Dr. William Hunter — p. 110—117].

former writers, particularly by Ambrose Paré, who relates a memorable instance of its good effects.

To his description of this case Dr. Hunter adds some remarks on the cellular membrane and its diseases – Haller had considered this membrane as the inorganic basis of all our organised and vascular solids; but Dr. Hunter, in this paper, observes, that as the inorganic stamina of the human body are too minute to be seen, it is impossible to determine their real nature with certainty; but he affirms, that all its visible parts are of a vascular texture.

He remarks, that the cellular membrane is of two kinds, reticular and adipose; and he differs from former anatomists, who had supposed, that the oil of the adipose membrane is lodged in the same cavities as the waters of the anasarca.

Wherever there is fat in the human body, he thinks there is a particular organisation or glandular apparatus superadded to the reticular membrane, consisting of vesicles for lodging the animal oil, as well as vessels fitted for its secretion; so that he compares the marrow in the bones to the glandular or follicular parts of the adipose membrane, and the net-work of bony fibres and laminae, which supports the marrow, to the reticular membrane that is mixed with and supports the adeps.

In treating the diseases of the cellular membrane, he mentions the anasarca. In cases of this sort the methods of discharging the water had been different. Some writers had recommended incisions of considerable length and depth; while others advised very small punctures. Dr. Hunter gives the preference to the latter, as being less painful, and less liable to inflammation and mortification. It seems that he had tried both these methods, one on each leg of the same patient, and by that means had clearly seen the advantage of the one method over the other.

In this paper we meet with a good description of the dropsy of the ovarium, a disease in which it had been proposed by some modern surgeons of great reputation to attempt a radical cure by incision and suppuration, or by the excision of the cyst. Dr. Hunter, who was always cautious in adopting any new operation where the chance of success seemed inadequate to the certainty of danger, clearly proves that excision can hardly be attempted; and that incision and suppuration can be recommended only under very particular circumstances.

His other papers in this second volume are, 1. An account of a diseased Tibia,[47] which shews that a callus will supply the place of a bone, and preserve the length and firmness of a limb, when the greatest part of the original bone is become useless, or thrown out by exfoliation; and 2. Remarks on the symphysis of the Ossa Pubis,[48] which he describes as a composition of two cartilages and a ligament, somewhat like the connecting substance between the bodies of the vertebrae. Several cases that had occurred to him sufficiently proved, that in lying-in women there may be a cavity in the symphysis of the ossa pubis, and he considered this observation as one step towards explaining why matter is sometimes collected there.

In the fourth volume he relates a case, which served to confirm his own and M. de Haller's theory concerning the insensibility of tendons;[49] and in that and the fifth volumes he communicated his observations on the Retroverted Uterus.[50] This disease, although it had been mentioned by M. Gregoire in his lectures at

Paris, and my friend, M. Peyrilhe, the learned author of a History of Surgery*, thinks he has discovered some traces of it in the writings of the ancients, was certainly not understood till Dr. Hunter described it, first in his lectures in 1754, and afterwards in one of the volumes of the work in question, since which it has been generally known. It is worthy of observation, however, that within two years before the publication of that volume two pregnant women had lost their lives by this accident, in London. In both of these instances experienced practitioners saw with regret in the dead body what they might have easily cured in the living, if they had made a very obvious discovery in proper time.

The sixth volume, which is now in the press, will contain three papers written by Dr. Hunter. In one of these he describes three cases, by way of supplement to an instance communicated by Dr. Pulteney, of an extraordinary conformation of the heart. In the second paper he relates the history of an obstinate disease of the stomach cured by the use of milk in small quantities; and in the third he treats of the uncertainty of the signs of murder in the case of bastard children.[51]

About the years 56 or 57 Dr. H-r joined his brother with him in the Lectures, giving him such Lectures as best suited a beginner in teaching, and giving him more and more of the Lectures as teaching became more familiar to him, which continued till the year 60, when his brother was made surgeon to the army and went in the expedition against Belle Isle in the Spring 61; and that the practical part of anatomy, as also the dissections for the winter courses 60 and 61 might be carried on, his Brother ingaged Mr. Hewson, then his House Pupil to perform that business for him, and he gave him the profits of the dissecting room (which was J.H.- emoluments) for Mr. Hewson's trouble. His Brother also recommended Mr. Hewson as a future assistant, but so much was Dr. H. attached to the habit of having his brother dissect for him, that he took the resolution of giving no more Lectures, and took a kind of fair well at the end of his spring course 61;[52] but the winter following he was solicitated by a number of Pupils to continue and as a number of his former Pupils had a right to a continuation, having paid for several courses to come, he resolved to give one course gratis, in which Mr. Hewson again assisted. For this course the Pupils joined and had a genteel piece of Plate [Plate VI] made with proper devices upon it.[53] Finding he could now go on with his Lectures, he in the Winter 62 and 63 gave his usual courses, assisted by Mr. Hewson as before, and afterwards took him as a Partner.

In 1762 we find him warmly engaged in controversy, supporting his claim to different anatomical discoveries, in a work entitled Medical Commentaries, the style of which is correct and spirited. As an excuse for the tardiness with which he brought forth this work, he observes in his introduction, that it required a good deal of time, and he had little to spare; that the subject was unpleasant, and therefore he was very seldom in the humour to take it up.

In this publication he confined himself chiefly to a dispute with the present learned professor of anatomy at Edinburgh, concerning injections of the testicle, the ducts of the lachrymal gland, the origin and use of the lymphatic vessels, and absorption by veins. He likewise defended himself against a reproach thrown upon him by Professor Monro, senior, by giving a concise account of a controversy he was involved in with Mr. Pott, concerning the discovery of the Hernia Congenita. It was not long before Mr. Pott took occasion to give the public his account of the dispute;[54] and, in reply, Dr. Hunter added a supplement to his Commentaries.[55]

* Histoire de la Chirurgie depuis son origine jusqu'à nos jours. Vol. II 4 Paris 1780.

It has been observed of anatomists that they are all liable to the error of being severe on each other in their disputes. Dr. Hunter, whose own writings* afford us this remark, very pleasantly adds, that for anything we know, the passive submission of dead bodies, their common objects, may render them less able to bear contradiction. "It is remarkable", says he, "that there is scarce a considerable character in anatomy that is not connected with some warm controversy. Anatomists have ever been engaged in contention. And indeed, if a man has not such a degree of enthusiasm, and love of the art, as will make him impatient of unreasonable opposition, and of encroachment upon his discoveries and his reputation, he will hardly become considerable in anatomy, or in any other branch of natural knowledge."

"These reflections afford some comfort to me, who unfortunately have been already engaged in two public disputes. I have imitated some of the greatest characters, in what is commonly reckoned their worst part; but I have also endeavoured to be useful; to improve and diffuse the knowledge of anatomy: and surely it will be allowed here, that if I have not been serviceable to the public in this way, it has not been for want of diligence or love of the service.†"

With regard to the injection of the testicle it may be remarked, that Dr. Monro filled the *tubuli testis* with mercury in 1753; and that Dr. Hunter proves his having shewed a preparation‡ of this kind at his lectures in 1752; but that Haller has since claimed the merit of having made and published this discovery so early as the year 1745.§

The ducts of the lachrymal gland after the discovery of them in the ox, by Stenon, had been often observed both in that animal and in the sheep. Santorini and Winslow had even seen and described them in the human subject; but some of the most distinguished modern anatomists had sought for them in vain, so that their existence in man was still a subject of dispute when Dr. Hunter began to teach anatomy.

It appears that at his lectures in 1747 he introduced bristles into the ducts of this gland in the human subject. Dr. Monro did the same thing in 1753. The reputation that could be derived from this circumstance, was hardly adequate to the warmth with which it was claimed by either of the disputants. It could not be the reputation of a first discovery, it was merely the credit of having demonstrated that which had escaped the penetration of Morgagni and Haller.

In the dispute concerning the origin and use of the lymphatic vessels, the eagerness of the contending parties was perhaps more excusable. The discovery was extremely interesting to the practice of physic and surgery, and the emulation of two anatomists who disputed with each other the honour of the invention, would naturally be in proportion to the importance of the subject.[56]

---

* Supplement to the First part of Medical Commentaries. [p 1.]
† Supplement to the [first part of] Medical Commentaries. [p 1.]
‡ Dr. Hunter acknowledges that it was Mr. Henry Watson who first shewed him the ducts coming out of the *testis* to form the *epididymis,* in a preparation where he had traced them by dissection with great accuracy. See Med. Com. p.2.
§ "Hunterus se anno 1752 testum cum suis vasis argento vivo replevisse monet; nos anno 1745 descripseramus, et in programmate Winklerianae disputationi addito, et in Philos. Trans." Halleri *Biblioth. Anatom.*

Dr. Hunter, in his account of the controversy, observes, that when he began to give lectures, the most commonly received opinion concerning the lymphatic veins was, that they were a continuation of lymphatic arteries; but that he, on the contrary, was led to consider them as a system of absorbing vessels, which begin from all the internal and external surfaces of the body.[57]

It was at that time generally allowed that all the surfaces of the body are bibulous, or provided with absorbent vessels, by which mercury applied to the skin, collections of water in the breast, belly or in the cellular membrance, &c are occasionally taken up and conveyed into the circulation. That the lymphatic veins perform this office, he thought probable, from having observed that he had not been able to inject them like other veins, by filling the arterial system; and from having sometimes remarked in injecting, that they were immediately filled with wax, when the arteries burst, and the wax was effused into the cellular membrane. But what appeared to him to be the most striking argument in support of his opinion was the analogy between the lymphatics and the lacteals. These two systems were to all appearance, the same in their coats, in their valves, in their manner of ramifying, in their passage through the lymphatic or conglobate glands, and in their termination in the thoracic duct. As they were perfectly similar, in every other respect, he supposed them to be so in their origin and use. The lacteals were known to begin from the surface of the intestines, and to be the absorbants of those parts. Hence he concluded, that there was no difference between them but in their names, and that the same vessels were called *lacteals* in the intestines and lymphatics in the other parts of the body. This doctrine explained the use of valves in the lymphatics. In other veins, the fluid was supposed to move onward by an impetus received in the arterial system; but the case could not be the same in vessels that inbibe a fluid from a surface. – These ideas concerning the lymphatics were farther confirmed by the absorption and progress of the veneral poison.

Such were the opinions maintained by Dr. Hunter in his lectures in the year 1746. Dr. Munro in his Inaugural Dissertation*, printed in 1755, introduced several arguments to prove that the valvular lymphatic vessels, through the whole body, are a system of absorbent veins, and that they do not proceed from the branches of arteries as was the common opinion: and two years afterwards in a work on lymphatics†, published at Berlin, he treats fully of their origin, structure and use, and quotes many of the latest writers to prove that his opinions on this subject were new.

Neither Dr. Hunter or Dr. Munro seem to have been aware that the main points for which they contended are to be found in an abridgement of anatomy‡ published at Paris so early as the year 1726 by M. Noguez, a French anatomist. This work, which is at present but little known, contains several passages that

* Dissertatio Inauguralis de Testibus et Semine in variis animalibus.
† De Venis Lymphaticis valvulosis et de earum imprimis origine.
‡ L'Anatomie du Corps de l'homme en abrégé; par M. Noguez, Medecin du Roy, et Demonstrateur d'histoire naturelle au Jardin Royal, 8vo Paris. 2nd edition 1726 — The first edition of this work, published in 1723, was little more than a translation of Keil's anatomy, but this second edition contains many observations peculiar to the author, and, among others, those which I have quoted, relative to the lymphatics.

have been overlooked* by succeeding writers, but which clearly prove that the author was not unacquainted with the absorbing office of the lymphatic veins, and their analogy to the lacteals.

In the eighth chapter of the third part of his work, M. Noguez, after having given a good account of the lacteals and their valves, and likewise of the thoracic duct, describes the lymphatics in the following terms: "La structure des vaisseaux lymphatiques et la manière de les demontrer sont les memes que dans les veines lactées . . . Les vaisseaux lymphatiques sont des vaisseaux tres petits; minces, transparens, qui renferment ordinairement une liqueur aqueuse qu'on appelle lymphe...on les trouve d'ordinaire à la surface des parties, sur tout du foye. Leur structure at leur substance ne different point des veines lactées. Ils ont beaucoup de valvules qui sont doubles et semi-lunaire, et qui sont d'un grand usage pour faciliter le mouvement progressif de la lymphe. Ruysch les a parfaitement bien decrites et demontrées. Il en nait de presque toutes les parties du corps, ou peut-etre de toutes les parties: la chose est encore indecise... Pour les demontrer il faut lier la vein thoracique, la veine cave, ou quelqu'autre gros tronc dans un animal vivant, ou tué depuis peu; on souffle ensuite dans les veines, ou dans les arteres, ou dans les tuyaux excretoires des visceres.... Il y a des glandes qu'on appelle *conglobées*, ou les vaisseaux lymphatiques aboutissent, et qui servent d'entre-pots".† He allows the existence of lymphatic arteries which exhale a subtile vapour or lymph, but he is careful to distinguish these from the *lymphatic veins*, which he considers as *absorbents*. "Les premiers" – says he – "naissent des extremitez arterieles, comme dans l'oeil, à la peau: on les nomment arteres lymphatiques, qui peut-être ne sont autre chose que les conduits excretoires d'une lymphe tres subtile, ou de la matiere de la transpiration. Les seconds vaisseaux lymphatiques sont veineux; ils reportent la lymphe dans les vaisseaux sanguins ou dans les veines; il y'en a dans toutes les parties du corps; ils repompent la matiere lymphatique qui s'evacue par les premiers, on peut les nommer conduits absorbans."‡ – There is certainly a great difference between

* I am aware that M. Noguez is one of the authors quoted by Mr. Hewson in his description of the lymphatic system; but Mr. Hewson makes no mention of those parts of M. Noguez's descriptions which relate to the analogy of the lymphatic veins to the lacteals, their difference from what were considered as lacteal arteries, or the means of demonstrating them.

†"The structure of the lymphatic vessels and the manner of demonstrating them are the same as in the lacteal veins . . . The lacteal vessels are very minute vessels; thin, transparent, and usually containing a watery liquor called lymph . . . They are commonly found on the surface of parts particularly of the liver. In their structure and composition they are the same as the lacteal veins. They have a great number of valves which are double and semi-lunar, and which are of great utility to facilitate the progressive motion of the lymph. Ruysch has described and demonstrated them perfectly well. They arise from almost all parts of the body or perhaps from every part; but this is as yet undetermined . . . To demonstrate them, we must first tie the thoracic duct, the vena cava or some other large trunk in a living animal, or one recently killed; and then blow into the veins or the arteries, or the excretory ducts of the viscera — There are glands called *conglobate*, where the lymph vessels enter, and which serve as reservoirs".

‡The first arise from the extremities of arteries as in the eye and in the skin. These may be called lymphatic arteries, and are perhaps no other than the excretory ducts of a very subtile lymph, or of the matter of perspiration. The second lymphatic vessels are venous, and carry back the lymph into the blood vessels or veins. They are met with in all parts of the body. *They suck up the lymphatic fluid, which is evacuated by the former and may be called absorbing vessels.*

this state of the discovery, and the progress that has since been made in it by injecting the lymphatic veins with mercury, tracing their origin and course in different parts of the body, explaining their structure and use, and applying the doctrine of absorption to pathology. For these improvements we are indebted to Dr. Hunter, Dr. Monro, Mr. Hewson, and other modern anatomists, but the passages I have just now quoted are sufficient to shew, that in a history of the absorbent system our obligations to M. Noguez ought not to be forgotten.

Speaking of dislocations* Dr. Hunter delivers what he supposed at the time to be a new doctrine, viz. that when a luxation is produced by violence in a healthy state, the capsular ligament is lacerated. But it has since been observed† that a similar opinion was adopted long ago by Petit. *He was I believe the first that introduced the present practice of setting a dislocated shoulder by first raising the arm and making the distention in that direction.*

In the course of his work Dr. Hunter takes occasion to treat† of the insensibility of the dura mater, periosteum, tendons, and ligaments. On this subject he professes to have delivered nearly the same doctrine in his lectures in 1746 as was afterwards published by Haller in 1752.‡ The just claim, however, of Haller to the thanks of the world for this discovery, as he made it fairly, and was the first who communicated it to the public, has never been disputed. It deserves to be remarked, however, that Dr. Hunter differs in some respects from Haller, who has gone too far, he thinks, in concluding that these parts have absolutely no *sense of* feeling; and who seems to have been led into an error in surgery, by supposing that wounds and punctures of tendons and ligaments, and penetrating wounds in the joints, are attended with as little danger as similar wounds in fleshy parts. Dr. Hunter very prudently cautions his readers against cutting into the cavity of a joint, unless there be very urgent reason for so dangerous a practice.

What he says of absorption by veins is founded chiefly on experiments made and related by his brother, Mr. John Hunter, and which, in his opinion, prove that in the human body the red veins do not absorb. *The experiments went to prove that no veins in any animal absorbed.*

With regard to the *hernia congenita* Dr. Hunter acknowledges that he first learned from Mr. Sharpe, in 1748, that cases of rupture sometimes occur, where the intestine is found in the same sac, and in contact with the *testis.* The truth of this he afterwards confirmed by his own observation, but till he read the account of the *hernia congenita* in Haller's *opuscula pathologica*§, he had constantly accounted for this phenomenon by supposing that the hernial sac had been lacerated. *Long before Hallers publication Dr. H. opened a child and found the Testicles within the abdomen and mentioned it to his Brother, but considered it as an uncommon circumstance, and I believe thought no more of it, till Hallers publication, nor did he then choose to claim it then.* He now engaged his brother to prosecute inquiries on this subject, and to this

---

* Medical Comm. Chap. 7.

† Kirkland's Obs. on Fractures, etc. p. 48.

‡ Traite des Maladies des Os. tom 1. p. 46.

§This work was published in 1754, but the account of the hernia congenita had appeared in a separate publication in 1749 and Haller made the discovery so early as 1747.

circumstances we are indebted for the "Observations* on the stage of the *testis* in the foetus, and on the hernia congenita, by Mr. John Hunter" which are published in the Medical Commentaries.[58]

Soon after the act, for giving the bodies of those who were hanged for murder to the company of Surgeons, he was appointed to read Lectures on one of those subjects, and gave umbrage to the Master and others, because he would have his brother dissect the parts for him.[59]

No man was ever more tenacious than Dr. Hunter of what he conceived to be his anatomical rights. This was particularly evinced in the year 1780, when his brother communicated to the Royal Society a discovery he had made twenty-five years before relative to the structure of the placenta, the communication between it and the uterus, and the vascularity of the spongy chorion.[60]

At the next meeting of the Society, a letter was read in which Dr. Hunter put in his claim to the discovery in question. This letter was followed by a reply from Mr. John Hunter, and here† the dispute then ended, *but in the year 87 [1786] Mr. J. Hunter published the discovery in his book entitled "Observations on certain parts of the animal oeconomy".*

In the year 17   he was imployed to lay the Princess of Brunswick, and his manner pleased the Dowger Princess of Wales and Lady Bute that they both recommended him to the Queen.[61]

In 1762, when our present amiable queen became pregnant, Dr. Hunter was consulted; and two years afterwards‡ he had the honour to be appointed Physician Extraordinary to her Majesty. In courts, where interest too often prevails over merit, appointments of this sort are not always conferred on persons of the greatest abilities. But it is certain that Dr. Hunter owed his nomination to this important office solely to his own well-earned reputation, and his assiduity and uniform success in the discharge of it shewed how well he deserved it.

About this time his avocations were so numerous that he became desirous of lessening his fatigue, and having noticed the ingenuity and assiduous application of the late Mr. William Hewson, F.R.S.,§ who was then one of his pupils, he engaged him first as an assistant and afterwards as a partner in his lectures. This connection continued till the year 1770, when some disputes happened which terminated in a separation. *In this dispute Mr. Hewson showed great indelicacy, pursued*

---

*Nos quidem testes in abdomine foetus habitare serius in scrotum descendere vidimus, et aliquando peritonaeum foramine patuisse, per quod testis exiret. Accuratius haec Johannes Hunter, Gulielmi frater, exposuit addidit, ut debilis cellulosa tela cedat, testem transmittat, peritonaeum vero supra transitum confirmet. Haec bonis iconibus exprimit." Halleri *Biblioth. Anatom.* tom 11. p. 363.

†These papers, though not published by the Society, are preserved in their archives. [Royal Society L + P vii, 138.]

‡1764.

§Of the life of this ingenious anatomist no account has been printed, till my learned friend Dr. Hahn, professor of physic in the university of Leyden, prefixed some anecdotes of him to a Latin translation of his works lately published in that city, but which I have not yet seen. These anecdotes are contained in the following letter with which Mr. Hewson's widow favoured me, in reply to one I had addressed to her at the suggestion of our common friend Mr. Watson, F.R.S. This letter I transmitted to Dr. Hahn, who tells me that he has given it entire in a Latin translation; and it affords so affectionate and just a tribute to the memory of Mr. Hewson, that I am persuaded my readers will be pleased to see it preserved here in its original form.

Sir,

I should think myself bound to grant any request introduced with Mr. Watson's name; but that which you make in the letter I received yesterday needed no such introduction. A tribute paid to the memory of Mr. Hewson is highly gratifying to me, and I can have no employment that will give me more satisfaction than that of assisting in any degree to the spreading of his fame.

You say you are not acquainted with the general history of Mr Hewson's life, and you speak of him in terms which shew you are not unacquainted with his character. Had you been among the number of his friends, you would bear testimony to his private virtues, which rendered him no less dear to his family and associates, than his talents made him respectable in the world.

Mr. Hewson was born at Hexham in Northumberland, on the 14th of November, O.S. 1739. He received the rudiments of his education at a grammar school in that town, under the Rev. Mr. Brown. His father was a surgeon and apothecary in the place, and much respected in that neighbourhood. With him Mr. Hewson acquired his first medical knowledge. Being ambitious to increase that knowledge, he placed himself first under an eminent surgeon in Newcastle (Mr. Lambert) and afterwards resided for some time at London, Edinburgh and Paris. His subsequent acquirements are sufficient to prove, that he visited those places with a true love of science and desire of attaining eminence in his profession.

I became acquainted with him in the year 1768. He was at that time in partnership with Dr. Hunter. Some similarity in our dispositions created a mutual esteem, and the equality of our situations made our union desirable in point of prudence. I had five months the start of him in age, no pretentions to beauty, nor any splendid fortune; yet I believe he was satisfied with the choice he made. We were married July 10th 1770. I brought him two sons. The elder was just three years old when Mr Hewson died, which was on the first of May, 1774, and I was delivered of a daughter on the ninth of August following. His last moments of recollection were embittered by the idea of leaving me with three children but scantily provided for. The trial of my fortitude was different; the loss of affluence I did not feel for myself, and I thought I could bring up my children not to want it. However, by the death of an aunt, who left me her fortune, I became reinstated in easy circumstances and am enabled to give a liberal education to my children, who I hope will prove worthy of the stock from which they grew and do honour to the name of Hewson.

Mr. Hewson's mother is still living at Hexham and has one daughter, the youngest and only remaining child of eleven.

His father died in 1767; and having had so large a family, it will be readily supposed he could not give much to his son, so that Mr. Hewson's advancement in life was owing to his own industry.

A better son and husband, or a fonder father than Mr. Hewson, never existed. He was honoured with the friendship of many respectable persons now living, and the late Sir John Pringle[63] shewed him singular marks of regard.

Mr. Hewson's manners were gentle and engaging; his ambition was free from ostentation, his prudence was without meanness, and he was more covetous of fame than of fortune.

You will, I trust, readily forgive me, if I have been more prolix than you desired. It would be no easy matter for me to relate bare facts without some comment upon such a subject.

I am, SIR,

Kensington   Your most obedient humble servant,
Aug. 30, 1782.   Mary Hewson.

To this letter I take the liberty to add that the writer of it, whose sentiments do her so much honour, is the lady[64] to whom Dr. Franklin has addressed several of his letters on Philosophical subjects, and likewise his scheme for a new Alphabet and reformed mode of Spelling, published in the collection of his Political, Miscellaneous and Philosophical pieces.

it with great rancor and self conceit, and endeavoured to make a party affair of it, purposely making friends with those he knew to be Dr. H's enemies and even telling private conversations. When Mr. Hewson gave his first course, he gave professedly a public Lecture against Dr. Hunter, which obliged Dr. Hunter to defend himself. In his course he advanced some new observations he had acquired when under Dr. H. roof and patronage without ever having acquainted Dr. H. with them.[62] Mr. Hewson was succeeded in the partnership by Mr. Cruickshank, whose anatomical abilities are deservedly respected.

In 1767* Dr. Hunter was elected a Fellow of the Royal Society, and the year following communicated to that learned body observations on the bones†, commonly supposed to be elephant's bones, which had been found near the river Ohio in America.

Naturalists had entertained very different opinions concerning fossil ivory, and the large teeth and bones dug up in different parts of the world. When they were clearly ascertained to be parts of animals (for at first this was doubted) a dispute arose to what animal they belonged. The more general opinion was, that they were the bones of an elephant; but this was liable to great objections. The bones were observed to be larger than those of the elephant, and it was thought strange that elephants should have been formerly so numerous in western countries where they are no longer natives, and in cold countries, Serbia particularly, where they cannot now live.

Of late years the same sort of tusks and teeth with some other larger bones have been found in considerable numbers near the banks of the Ohio in North America. The French academicians became possessed of some specimens of them, and having compared them with the bones of real elephants, and with those which had been brought to France from Siberia, determined with an appearance of truth on their side that they were elephant bones.

This part of natural knowledge appeared to Dr. Hunter to be very curious and interesting, inasmuch as it seemed to concur with many other phenomena in proving that in former times some astonishing change must have happened to this terraqueous globe; that the highest mountains in most countries, now known, must have lain for many ages in the bottom of the sea; and that this earth must have been so changed with respect to climates, that countries, which are now intensely cold must have been formerly inhabited by animals that are now confined to the warm climates.

After *getting his brother to examine* a great number of these teeth and bones, *his opinion was that they were not elephants, but must belong to some animal which was carniverous,* and carefully reading what had been published on this subject by M.M. de Buffon and D'Aubenton‡, Dr. Hunter was convinced that the supposed American elephant was an animal of another species which naturalists were unacquainted with. He imagined further that this *animal incognitum* would prove to be the supposed elephant of Siberia and other parts of Europe, and that the real elephant would be found to have been in all ages a native of Asia and Africa only. In the course of this inquiry having procured one of these fossil tusks to be cut

---

* April 30.
† Philos. Transactions, vol 58. [1768 p.34-45.]
‡Histoire Natur. tom XI. & Mem. de l'Acad. des Sciences, 1762.

through and polished, he discovered that true or genuine ivory is the production of two different animals and not of the elephant alone.

This was not the only subject of natural history of which Dr. Hunter employed his pen; for in a subsequent volume* of the Philosophical Transactions, we find him offering his remarks on some bones found in the rock of Gibraltar, and which he proves to have belonged to some quadruped. In the same work† likewise he published an account of the Nyl-ghau, an Indian animal, not described before, and which, from its strength and swiftness, promised to be a useful acquisition to this country.

In 1768‡ Dr. Hunter became a Fellow of the Society of Antiquaries, and the same year at the institution of a Royal Academy of Arts, he was appointed by his majesty to the office of Professor of Anatomy. This appointment opened a new field for his abilities, and he engaged in it as he did in every other pursuit of his life, with unabating zeal. He now adapted his anatomical knowledge to the objects of painting and sculpture, and the novelty and justness of his observations proved at once the readiness and extent of his genius.[65]

In January 1781, he was unanimously elected to succeed the late Dr. John Fothergill as president of this society.[66] He was one of those to whom we are indebted for its establishment, and our grateful acknowledgements are due to him for his zealous endeavours to promote the liberal views of this institution, by rendering it a source of mutual improvement, and thus making it ultimately useful to the public.

As his name and talents were known and respected in every part of Europe, so the honours conferred on him were not limited to his own country. In 1780 the Royal Medical Society at Paris elected him one of their foreign associates; and in 1782 he received a similar mark of distinction from the Royal Academy of Sciences in that city.

We come now to the most splendid of Dr. Hunter's medical publications, the Anatomy of the Human Gravid Uterus. The appearance of this work, which had been begun so early as the year 1751 (at which time ten of the thirty-four plates it contains were completed) was retarded till the year 1775 [1774], only by the author's desire of sending it into the world with fewer imperfections. Something concerning the progress of this work, and of the zeal with which it was prosecuted, may be collected from different parts of his letter to professor Monro, Senior, in the Supplement to his Medical Commentaries,[67] "On the 11th of February – he says – I was so fortunate as to meet with a Gravid Uterus, to which, from that time, all the hours have been dedicated which have been at my own disposal. I have been busy in injecting, dissecting, preserving, and shewing it, and in planning and superintending drawings and plaster casts of it.[68] *(He was probably the first that made molds of parts of the human body, and to make them appear as like nature as possible he had them painted from the subject. This mode of representation has been copy'd by most since.)* I have already made five very capital drawings from this subject. They and some more, shall be engraved by the best masters, as soon as possible, and then the whole shall be published. My first and original intention,

*Vol. 60. [1770, p. 414—416.]
†Phil. Trans. vol 61 [1771 p. 170—181.]
‡Jan. 14.

you know, was to have published ten plates only; but thinking the work imperfect, I waited patiently for more opportunities of adding supplemental figures. Sixteen plates were finished on this plan several years ago; but still I was dissatisfied with the work, as being incomplete; and in spite of the importunity of many friends, I kept it from the public."

Opportunities of dissecting the Human Gravid Uterus occur but seldom. It was probably owing to this circumstance that this part of anatomy had been less successfully cultivated than some others. Few, or none, of the anatomists, had met with a sufficient number of subjects, either for investigating, or demonstrating the principal circumstances of Utero-gestation in the human species.

In the course of thirty years, by great diligence, and the assistance of many friends, Dr. Hunter procured in this metropolis so many opportunities of studying the Gravid Uterus, as to be enabled to exhibit, by figures, all the principal changes that occur in the nine months of pregnancy.[69]

This great work was dedicated to the King. In his preface to it we find the author very candidly acknowledging that in most of the dissections he had been assisted by his brother, Mr. John Hunter, "whose accuracy – he adds – in anatomical researches is so well known, that to omit this opportunity for thanking him for that assistance would be in some measure to disregard the future reputation of the work itself". He likewise confesses his obligations to the ingenious artists who made the drawings and engravings, "but particularly to Mr. Strange, not only for having by his hand secured a sort of immortality to two of the plates, but for having given his advice and assistance in every part with a steady and disinterested friendship".[70]

The plates are not all equally interesting or beautiful, but I believe their accuracy has never been disputed. The four first engravings by Strange and Ravenet, and those of the Ovum in early pregnancy by Worlidge are justly admired for their elegance.

In this work Dr. Hunter first delineated the Retroverted Uterus, and the *Membrana decidua reflexa* or that part of the spongy chorion which is reflected over the foetus, and for the discovery of which we are indebted to him.

After the last plate was finished, he had an opportunity of procuring drawings to be made from a younger embryo than he had till then seen, and likewise from a very curious case of a conception in the Fallopian tube, which confirmed two opinions that he had before entertained concerning the Gravid Uterus. It shewed, that the enlargement of the impregnated Uterus does not happen mechanically from the increasing bulk of its contents; and it proved, at the same time, that the spongy chorion, or *membrana decidua,* belongs to the Uterus, and not to the Ovum or that part of the conception which is brought from the Ovarium. These drawings he intended to have offered to the public in the way of a supplemental plate, or with the description of the Gravid Uterus, a work which he did not live to publish, but which he seems to have almost completely prepared for the press. This description* was intended to be printed in quarto, as

---

* Some idea may be formed of the plan of this intended work from the following view of its contents, and their arrangement, written by the author himself. "Size of the Uterus at Nine Months. ——— Figure. ——— Situation. ——— Ligaments, Tubes and Ovaria. ——— Thickness of the Uterus. ——— Blood vessels. ——— Lymphatics and Nerves. ———

an illustration of his plates.[71] The two works united would certainly convey as accurate an idea of the anatomy of the Gravid Uterus as can be acquired without the actual dissection of pregnant women. This anatomical description of the Gravid Uterus was not the only work which Dr. Hunter had in contemplation to give to the public. He had long been employed in collecting and arranging materials for a history of the various concretions that are formed in the human body. In this work he intended to comprehend not only urinary and biliary concretions, but likewise those which take place in the salivary glands, pancreas, prostate, etc. of the urinary and biliary concretions he meant to treat at considerable length, because they are by much the most common; of the others, as being less frequent, he intended to treat more slightly.

He seems to have advanced no farther in the execution of this design, than to have nearly completed that part of it which relates to urinary and biliary concretions. Of these he describes the mechanical properties, as their specific gravity, colour, size, shape, etc. and their chymical properties discoverable by experiments. He considers likewise their mode of growth, *which he took from John Hunter's treatis on the teeth,*[72] and adds a short account of their pathology. It is probable that he meant to treat of the other concretions in the same way. This work was intended to be illustrated by engravings. The greater number of these were finished at his death and are executed with uncommon elegance.[73]

Amongst Dr. Hunter's papers have likewise been found two introductory lectures, which are written out so fairly, and with such accuracy, that he probably intended no farther correction of them before they should be given to the world.[74] In these lectures Dr. Hunter traces the history of anatomy from the earliest to the present times, along with the general progress of science and the arts. He considers the great utility of anatomy in the practice of physic and surgery; gives the ancient divisions of the different substances composing the human body, which for a long time prevailed in anatomy; points out the most advantageous mode of cultivating this branch of natural knowledge; and concludes with explaining the particular plan of his own lectures.

Besides these manuscripts he has also left behind him a considerable number of cases of dissection; most of them relate to pregnant women, and they are written with tolerable accuracy.[75]

The same year in which the tables of the Gravid Uterus made their appearance, Dr. Hunter communicated to the Royal Society, an Essay on the origin of the Venereal Disease. In this paper he attempted to prove, that this dreadful malady was not brought from America to Europe by the crew of Columbus, as had been commonly supposed, although it made its first appearance about that period.

In order to support this opinion, Dr. Hunter pointed out several inaccuracies in Astruc's testimonies, which contradict his assertion that the venereal infection

Muscular Fibres. ——— Os Uteri. ——— Contents of the Uterus. ——— Navel String. — —— Placenta. ——— Membranes Amnios, Chorion, and Decidua. ——— Allantois and Urachus. ——— Liquor Amnii. ——— Foetus; its Situation, Size, Form, etc. ——— Of the Pregnant Uterus in the earlier Months. ——— How far back in Pregnancy my Observations go. ——— Substance of the Uterus softer, more vascular, and rather thicker. ——— The Conception then in the Fundus. ——— State of the Cervix Uteri. ——— State of the Os Uteri. ——— Uterus not tight or quite full. ——— Situation of the Ligaments of the Uterus. ——— Ovarium and Corpus Luteum."

first made its appearance between the years 1494 and 1496. In particular he observed, that Fulgosius, one of the writers to whom Astruc appeals, positively says, that this disease made its appearance two years before Charles the Eight's arrival in Italy, which would fix it to 1492. But the authority on which Dr. Hunter laid the greatest stress, was that of Peter Martyr*, a native of Italy, who went to Spain in 1487, and resided there till his death, which happened in 1525. His talents soon procured him the patronage of the court, and he was appointed one of the council for the direction of affairs in the West Indies. He was the intimate friend of Columbus, and besides other works was the author of a history of the Discovery of America. His letters, which were published after his death, are full of information about the New World, but no where does he take notice of the venereal disease being conveyed from thence, though he often speaks of that complaint as a new disease which had just made its appearance, and which he ascribes, agreeably to the philosophy of those times, to planetary influence. One of his letters, addressed to Arias Luritanus, professor of Greek at Salamanca, who was afflicted with this new disease, is dated 1489, which was before Columbus even sailed from Spain on his first voyage.

After this paper had been read to the Royal Society, Dr. Hunter, in conversation with the late Dr. Musgrave, was convinced that the testimony on which he placed his chief dependence was of less weight than he had at first imagined, as many of Martyr's letters afford the most convincing proofs of their having been written a considerable time after the period of their dates. He therefore very properly laid aside his intention of giving his Essay to the public.[76]

In the year 1777, Dr. Hunter joined with Mr. Watson in presenting to the Royal Society a short Account of the late Dr. Maty's Illness, and of the Appearances on Dissection;† and the year following he published his Reflections on the Section of the Symphysis Pubis. This Essay, which was first read by the author at one of the quarterly meetings of this Society, contains a great number of useful observations. By sending forth this work Dr. Hunter did not mean to raise a popular cry against this new practice, before it was well understood, for he thought that this would be unfair, and at the same time disrespectful to the ingenuity, and, no doubt, humane intentions, of Messieurs Sigault, Camper and Le Roy, the authors of the operation. All that he wished for was to see it received with caution, and finally approved or rejected upon solid ground, and at as little expense to human nature as possible.[77]

The merits of this invention have lately been more fully investigated by Dr. Osborn,‡ who has so clearly ascertained its inutility and danger that it will probably never be attempted in this country.

We must now go back a little in order of time to describe the origin and progress of Dr. Hunter's Museum, without some account of which the history of his life would be very incomplete.

---

* This writer must not be confounded with another of the same name, and likewise a native of Italy, who was professor of Divinity at Oxford, and died at Zurich in 1562.

†Phils. Trans. vol. 67. [1777 p. 608—613]

‡An Essay on Laborious Parturition; in which the division of the Symphysis Pubis is particulary considered. 8 vo. Lond. 1783.

When he began to practice midwifery, *he was like most other young beginners desirous of getting on in his profession, as also* he was desirous of acquiring a fortune sufficient to place him in easy and independent circumstances. *His Industry was attended with the desired success and soon became the most distinguished of his profession, and by his address he extended the practice of midwifery, reconciling it to many who before had a horror of men.* Before many years had elapsed he found himself in possession of a sum adequate to his wishes in this respect, and this he set apart as a resource of which he might avail himself whenever age or infirmities should oblige him to retire from business. I have heard him say, that he once took a considerable sum from this fund for the purposes of his museum, but that he did not feel himself perfectly at ease till he had restored it again.

About the year 64 or 65 he had acquired about £20000, and had long before that time given orders to a friend in Scotland, if any Estate could be had he would become a purchaser. About this time one offer'd which was to have cost £22000, but the Title did not please him, altho good. – Till now this money had accumulated to this sum, but since having had his mind turned towards the disposal of this money, and being disappointed in the purchase of the Estate, and having a collection of ores sent him from Cornwall by Lady St. Aubin he began soon to increase them; his mind now having taken another turn, for before this he held such collections in contempt and was always out of humor with his Brother who had begun a collection of ores with other parts of natural History. He now took a resolution of keeping always [£]20000 in the funds, and whatever he got over that sum should be laid out in that way. After he had obtained this competency, as his wealth continued to accumulate, he formed a laudable design of engaging in some scheme of public utility, and at first had it in contemplation to found an anatomical school in this metropolis. For this purpose, about the year 1765, during the administration of Mr. Grenville, he presented a memorial to that minister, in which he requested the grant of a piece of ground in the Mews for the scite of an anatomical theatre. Dr. Hunter undertook to expend seven thousand pounds on the building, and to endow a professorship of anatomy, in perpetuity. This scheme did not meet with the reception it deserved.[78] *It was at first proposed that he should have a piece of ground in the King's Mews which pleased him much but was afterward informed he could not have it there, and was offer'd ground in such places, as were unfit for a public school, he was by this refusal much hurt, and said he would take his collection to the university of Glasgow,[79] where he had been educated, which promis he seems never to have forgot, and indeed it is not to be wonder'd at, when we reflect that there was by no suceeding minister any attempt to make up the loss this country sustained by the illiberal treatment this country received from George Grenville.* In a conversation on this subject soon afterwards with the Earl of Shelburne, his Lordship expressed a wish that the plan might be carried into execution by subscription, and very generously requested to have his name set down for a thousand guineas. Dr. Hunter's delicacy would not allow him to adopt this proposal. He chose rather to execute it at his own expense, and accordingly purchased a spot of ground in Great Windmill-street, where he erected a spacious house to which he removed from Jermyn-street in 1770.[80]

In this building, besides a handsome amphitheatre and other convenient apartments for his lectures and dissections, there was one magnificent room fitted up with great elegance and propriety as a museum.

Of the magnitude and value of his anatomical collection, some idea may be formed when we consider the great length of years he employed in the making of anatomical preparations, and in the dissection of morbid bodies, added to the eagerness with which he procured additions from the collections of Sandys*, Hewson†, Falconar‡, Blackhall§ and others that were at different times offered for sale in this metropolis. His specimens of rare diseases were likewise frequently increased by presents from his medical friends and pupils, who, when anything of this sort occurred to them, very justly thought they could not dispose of it more properly than by placing it in Dr. Hunter's museum. Speaking of an acquisition in this way, in one of his publications he says, "I look upon every thing of this kind which is given to me, as a present to the public; and consider myself as thereby called upon to serve the public with more diligence." ‖

Before his removal to Windmill-street, he had confined his collection chiefly to specimens of human and comparative anatomy *(he had very few preparations in comparative anatomy, having always objected strongly against them)* and of diseases, but now he extended his views to fossils and likewise to the promotion of polite literature and erudition, *which he took up early.*[81]

In a short space of time he became possessed of "the most magnificent treasure of Greek and Latin books that has been accumulated by any person now living, since the days of Mead". This is the character given of the doctor's library by a learned and industrious writer¶, who records an anecdote*ff* which does honour to Dr. Hunter's skill in bibliography.

*See p. 8.

†See p. 18.

‡ Magnus Falconar, surgeon, was born at Cheltenham in Gloucestershire, in November 1751. He married a sister of Mr. Hewson, and succeeded him as a reader on anatomy in London. He died of a pulmonary consumption at Bristol, March 24, 1778, at the age of 24 years. He was a man of great application and dexterity, and a good speaker. The sale of his collection of anatomical preparations, which included those made by Mr. Hewson, produced upwards of nine hundred pounds.

§ Andrew Blackall, a young anatomist of great abilities, was a native of Ireland, and began to teach anatomy in London in 1778, soon after the death of Mr. Falconar. He died at Bristol Hot Wells, August 14, 1780 of a pulmonary consumption in his 27th year.

‖ Letter to Dr. Vaughan, prefixed to the Reflections relative to the operation of cutting the Symphysis of the Ossa Pubis.

¶ Edward Harwood, D.D. in the preface to the *first edition* of his View of the various editions of the Greek and Roman classics. In this preface the author acknowledges his obligations to Dr. Hunter for having been allowed free access to consult any curious editions he wanted to inspect in his museum. In a subsequent edition this and several other passages where Dr. Hunter's name occurs, are suppressed.[82]

ff"I have only to regret that I did not happen to see, till after the article of Theocritus was printed off, a very curious *editio princeps* of this poet in Dr. Hunter's museum, in which the doctor, upon carefully collating two copies, as he imagined of the same edition, printed at Venice, Gr. fol. 1495, discovered a material difference not noticed by any bibliographer. The Dr. ingeniously accounted for it, by supposing it to be printed from a mutilated manuscript, and that Aldus, after having disposed of a few copies of this imperfect edition, in the mean time meeting with a completer manuscript, supplied the deficiency of those copies which remained unsold, by printing two or three new sheets, and inserting them in the work. This curious circumstance relative to this edition of Theocritus, by Aldus, appears to have been unknown to the ingenious editor of the late Oxford edition of Theocritus, and will undoubtedly induce learned men to inspect this uncommon book." This is another of the passages omitted by Dr. Harwood in a late edition of his work.

A cabinet of ancient medals contributed likewise much to the richness of his museum. A description* of part of the coins, in this collection, struck by the Greek free cities, has lately been published by the doctor's learned friend Mr. Combe. In a classical dedication of this elegant volume to the queen, Dr. Hunter acknowledges his obligations to her majesty. In the preface some account is given of the progress of the collection, which has been brought together since the year 1770, with singular taste, and at the expense of upwards of twenty thousand pounds.

In 1781, the museum received a valuable addition of shells, corals and other subjects of natural history which had been collected by our late worthy president Dr. Fothergill, who gave directions by his will that his collection should be appraised after his death, and that Dr. Hunter should have the refusal of it at five hundred pounds under valuation. This was accordingly done, and Dr. Hunter purchased it for the sum of twelve hundred pounds.[83]

The fame of this museum spread throughout Europe. Few foreigners, distinguished for their rank or learning, visited this metropolis without requesting to see it.[84] Considered in a collective point of view it is perhaps without a rival.

Dr. Hunter, at the head of his profession, honoured with the esteem of his sovereign, and in the possession of everything that his reputation and wealth could confer, seemed now to have attained the summit of his wishes. But these sources of gratification were embittered by a deposition to gout, which harrassed him frequently during the latter part of his life, notwithstanding his very abstemious manner of living.

About ten years before his death his health was so much impaired, that, fearing he might soon become unfit for the fatigues of his profession, he began to think of retiring to Scotland. With this view he requested his friends Dr. Cullen and Dr. Baillie[85] to look out for a pleasant estate for him. A considerable one, and such as they thought would be agreeable to him, was offered for sale about that time in the neighbourhood of Alloa. A description of it was sent to him, and met with his approbation. The price was agreed on, and the bargain supposed to be concluded. But when the title deeds of the estate came to be examined by Dr. Hunter's counsel in London, they were found defective, and he was advised not to complete the purchase.[86] After this he found the expenses of his museum increased so fast, that he laid aside all thoughts of retiring from practice.

This alteration in his plan did not tend to improve his health. In the course of a few years the returns of his gout became by degrees more frequent, sometimes affecting his limbs and sometimes his stomach, but seldom remaining many hours in one part. Notwithstanding this valetudinary state, his ardour seemed to be unabated. In the last year of his life he was as eager to acquire new credit, and to secure the advantage of what he had before gained, as he could have been at the most enterprizing part of his life. At length, on Saturday the 15th of March, 1783, after having for several days experienced a return of wandering gout, he complained of great head-ache and nausea. In this state he went to bed, and for several days felt more pain than usual both in his stomach and limbs.

*Nummorum veterum populorum et urbium qui in museo Gulielmi Hunter affervantur descriptio figuris illustrata. Opera et studio Carli Combe, S.R. et SA. soc. 4 to Londini 1783.

On the Thursday following he found himself so much recovered that he determined to give the introductory lecture to the operations of surgery. It was to no purpose that his friends urged to him the impropriety of such an attempt. He was determined to make the experiment, and accordingly delivered the lecture, but towards the conclusion his strength was so exhausted that he fainted away, and was obliged to be carried to bed by two servants. The following night and day his symptoms were such as indicated danger, and on Saturday morning Mr. Combe, who made him an early visit, was alarmed on being told by Dr. Hunter himself, that during the night he had certainly had a paralytic stroke. As neither his speech nor his pulse were affected, and he was able to raise himself in bed, Mr. Combe encouraged him to hope that he was mistaken. But the event proved the doctor's idea of his complaint to be but too well founded; for from that time till his death, which happened on Sunday 30th March, he voided no urine without the assistance of the catheter, which was occasionally introduced by his brother; and purgative medicines were administered repeatedly without procuring a passage by stool. These circumstances, and the absence of pain, seemed to shew that the intestines and urinary bladder had lost their sensibility and power of contraction; and it was reasonable to presume that a partial palsy had affected the nerves distributed to those parts.

The latter moments of his life exhibited an instance of philosophical calmness and fortitude that well deserves to be recorded. Turning to his friend Mr. Combe, "If I had strength enough to hold a pen – said he – I would write how easy and pleasant a thing it is to die."

By his will, the use of his museum, under the direction of trustees, devolves to his nephew Matthew Baillie, B.A. and in the case of his death to Mr. Cruickshank for the term of thirty* years, at the end of which period the whole collection is bequeathed to the University of Glasgow.

The sum of eight thousand pounds sterling is left as a fund for the support and augmentation of the collection.[87]

The trustees are Dr. George Fordyce, Dr. David Pitcairne, and Mr. Charles Combe, to each of whom Dr. Hunter has bequeathed an annuity of twenty pounds for thirty years, that is, during the period in which they will be executing the purposes of the will.

Dr. Hunter has likewise bequeathed an annuity of one hundred pounds to his sister, Mrs. Baillie, during her life, and the sum of two thousand pounds to each of her two daughters. The residue of his estate and effects goes to his nephew, *but the paternal estate of Long Calderwood came to his brother, the Dr. having no right to dispose of it.*[88]

On Saturday the 5th of April, his remains were interred in the rector's vault of St. Jame's church, Westminster. *His pupils had such esteem for him that they all went into mourning.*

Of the person of Dr. Hunter, it may be observed, that he was regularly shaped, but of a slender make, *rather delicate altho a very healthy appearance* and rather below a middle stature.

---

* In his will Dr. Hunter had limited the term to twenty years, but in a codicil he afterwards extended it to thirty. [The collections were moved to Glasgow in 1807.]

There are several good *(bad)* portraits of him extant. One of these is an unfinished painting* by Zoffany [Plate VII], who has represented him in the attitude of giving a lecture on the muscles at the Royal Academy, surrounded by a group of academicians.[89] Of the engraved prints of him which have appeared, I give the preference to that executed by Collyer, from the portrait by Chamberlin[90] [Plate VIII], in the Council Chambers of the Royal Academy. It exhibits an accurate and striking resemblance of his features. *(All the portraits of him are too strongly marked, they represent him as vulgar, while his real appearance was genteel and delicate.)*

His manner of living was extremely simple and frugal, and the quantity of his food was small as well as plain.[91] He was an early riser and when business was over he was constantly engaged in his anatomical pursuits, or in his museum.

(He was not an early riser, rather indulged in his bed when he might, and [was] naturally indolent, loved ease and social company, but his good sense, and desire to be at the head of his profession, or whatever he undertook, made him active.)

It has been said that he was restrained by mere parsimony, from indulging in the luxuries and amusements which captivate the generality of people who reside in this great city. But he seems to have had no relish for them, and contrived to live, in the midst of a crowd, master of himself, and of his own pursuits. – It may with truth be asserted, that he never suffered his economy to interfere in matters where the dignity of his character, or the interest of science, were concerned. *He perhaps did not make sufficient alowance for the natural frailty of human nature, he pitied none who had been the cause of their own misery therefore seldom assisted such; but where there was real distress and not brought on by their own folly, he was very liberal, and in the quietest way possible.*

There was something very engaging in his manner and address, and he had such an appearance of attention to his patients when he was making his inquiries as could hardly fail to conciliate their confidence and esteem. – In consultation with his medical brethern, he delivered his opinions with diffidence and candour. – In familiar conversation he was chearful and unassuming.

All who knew him allow he possessed an excellent understanding, great readiness of perception, a good memory, and a sound judgment. To these intellectual powers he united uncommon assiduity and precision, so that he was admirably fitted for anatomical investigation.

As a teacher of anatomy he has been long and deservedly celibrated.– He was a good orator, and having a clear and accurate conception of what he taught, he knew how to place in distinct and intelligible points of view the most abstruse subjects of anatomy and physiology. Among other methods of explaining and illustrating his doctrines, he used frequently to introduce some apposite story or case that had occurred to him in his practice, and few men had acquired a more intersting fund of anecdotes of this kind, or related them in a more agreeable manner. He had the talent of infusing much of his ardour into his pupils, and if anatomical knowledge is more diffused in this country than formerly, we are indebted for this, in great measure, to his exertions.

---

*This picture is in the possession of Mr. Baillie. The portrait of Dr. Hunter is the only part of it that is finished. Of the other figures Mr. Zoffany had only traced the outlines, when he embarked for the East Indies.

To him, likewise, we owe much of the moderation and caution which now prevail amongst discreet, and intelligent practitioners of midwifery, in the use of instruments. "I admit – said he in one of his latest publications* – that the forceps may sometimes be of service, and may save either the mother or child. I have sometimes used it with advantage, and, I believe, never materially hurt a mother or child with it, because I always used it with fear and circumspection. Yet I am clearly of opinion, from all the information which I have been able to procure, that the forceps (midwifery instruments in general I fear) upon the whole, has done more harm than good." In his lectures he had uniformly delivered the same excellent sentiments.

How much he contributed to the improvement of medical science in general may be collected from the concise view we have taken of his writings.

The munificence he displayed in the cause of science has likewise a claim to our applause. – Persons of an invidious turn of mind who seek to depreciate his merit in this respect, may perhaps endeavour to trace the motive by which he was actuated, and ascribe to vanity what deserves rather to be considered as a commendable love of fame. It is certain that Dr. Hunter sacrificed no part of his time or his fortunes to voluptuousness, to idle pomp, or to any of the common objects of vanity that influence the pursuits of mankind in general. He seems to have been animated with a desire of distinguishing himself in those things which are in their nature laudable, and being a batchelor, and without views for establishing a family, he was at liberty to indulge his inclination. Let us, therefore, not with-hold the praise that is due to him; and at the same time let it be observed, that his temperance, his prudence, his persevering and eager pursuit of knowledge constitute an example which we may with advantage to ourselves, and to society, endeavour to imitate.

---

* Reflections relative to the operation of cutting the Symphysis of the Ossa Pubis.[92]

NOTES

1. In correspondence between the Cullen family and John Thomson when he was writing the life of William Cullen, it is made plain that the Duke of Hamilton had nothing to do with William Cullen starting in practice in Hamilton (Thomson/Cullen Papers, Glasgow University).

2. According to Dorothy Baillie, William Hunter's sister, it was a brother of William's mother who was influential in converting him to the opinions of Arius, that made it unsuitable for him to enter the church (Hunter-Baillie Papers, vol. 6, f.19).

3. James was in London by 1742 before James Douglas died. Letter from William Hunter to his mother, 3 June, 1742 (Hunter-Baillie Papers, vol. 2, f.3).

4. It cannot have been while James was in London in 1742-3 that he worked with Tobias Smollett on a play, for between 1739 and 1744 Smollett was serving as a naval surgeon in the West Indies. It is more likely that it was during the time that James was living at home, after having given up the practice of law, and while Smollett was apprenticed to a surgeon in Glasgow, before he went down to London in 1739.

5. It was possibly in 1738, not 1740, that Hunter went to Edinburgh University, for it was for the year 1738 that a William Hunter is recorded as attending Alexander Monro's anatomy lectures. No W. Hunter is recorded for 1739 or 1740 (Lists of Alexander Monro's pupils. Edinburgh University Manuscript Collection).

6. This date should be 1740. Letter from W. Hunter to unnamed correspondent, dated 6 November, 1740, after his arrival in London (Hunter-Baillie Papers, vol. 2, f.9).

7. *The Odes, Epodes and Carmen Seculare of Horace, translated into English prose as near the original as the different idioms of the Latin and English will allow.* Translated by David Watson (London, 1741).

8. Hunter-Baillie Papers, vol. 1, f.51.

9. James Douglas was, from its foundation in 1735, a Governor of St. George's Hospital.

10. James Wilkie, Scotsman, in 1720 appointed surgeon at the Westminster Hospital, also acted as salaried apothecary. Ceded from Westminster Hospital to become one of the founders and Senior Surgeon in Ordinary, St. George's Hospital. Resigned 1744 because of ill-health; died 1750.

11. James Douglas was married twice. Who his first wife was is not known, nor when she died, but it must have been before 1716, for her death is referred to in a letter to James Douglas, addressed to him in Fleet Street, from which he moved in 1716 (Glasgow University Library Gen. Ms. 505. f.26). Secondly, he married Martha Wilkes, daughter of Israel Wilkes and aunt of John Wilkes, the politician. By her he had at least three children, of whom Israel James is mentioned in a letter of William to his brother James (Houghton Library, Harvard University, Autograph File), in which he mentions 'my friend Mr. J. Douglas', who had been in poor health through

the winter of 1743/4. He probably died before 1752, for he was not mentioned in his mother's will. Martha-Jane died 1744, aged 26; it is thought that William Hunter became engaged to her. It was the second son, William George (1725-1755), whom William may have met while they were both in Edinburgh studying anatomy (for William George is recorded as a pupil of Alexander Monro in 1739), and to whom William was tutor. When William George died he was in debt. His nearest relative, a cousin, refused to administer the estate, and goods, chattels and credits were granted to Richard Holmes, Esq., a creditor (P.R.O., P.C.S. Adom. 1755). A second daughter, but it is not known whether she was a child of the first or second marriage, was the wife of Dr. Owen, partner of John Douglas, James's brother. Letter from William to James Hunter, September 1743 (Hunter-Baillie Papers, vol. 2. f.5).

12. No such 'notes of hand' are now to be found.

13. It was James Douglas's wish that Hunter should study anatomy in Paris.

> At his death I had mournings and a ring from Mrs. Douglas. Then I was told that on his death-bed he acquainted his family he had promised that I should go to Paris, and that I must go.

William Hunter to his mother, 3 June, 1742 (Hunter-Baillie Papers, vol. 2, f.3).

14. Hunter studied with Antoine Ferrein. (Notes by Hunter of his lectures are in Hunterian Ms. 216) and with Henri François le Dran (George Arnaud, *Memoires de Chirurgie.* Paris, 1768).

15. Alexander Monro (primus), *An expostulatory espistle to William Hunter M.D.* (Edinburgh, 1762).

16. This refers to whether or not Alexander Monro, secundus, had learnt from William Hunter's lectures Hunter's ideas on the function of the lymphatic system.

17. Though Hunter doubtless had been making preparations for himself, he certainly acquired some, if not all, of James Douglas's considerable collection. Douglas himself refers to his collection both of 'diseased bones.....pretty nearly complete' and of 'all the possible ways of getting into the Humane Bladder', and it is also referred to by John Freind in his *History of Physic* (1725) and by Aston Warner, who in *Dr. Littlejohn's proposal....for the more effectual cure of such seamen as may have ruptures* (London, 1734), describes it as 'the best collection of practically useful anatomical preparations (acquired, prepared, and preserved at vast expense, fatigue and care) that either is or ever was in the possession of any single man'. Specimens of James Douglas can be identified in the Hunterian Collection.

18. The Society of Naval Surgeons was not founded till January 1746/7, after Hunter had started lecturing in the autumn of 1746, so he could not have first lectured at the invitation of that Society (Peachey *loc. cit.* p.84). William Hunter made notes of a *Course of Chyrurgical Operations performed before the Society of Naval Surgeons* by Sam. Sharp of Guy's Hospital, March, 1746, – i.e. March, 1746/7 (Hunterian Ms. 216), so that the first course to the Naval Surgeons was given by Sharp. Therefore, William Hunter's first anatomy

course was in no way connected with the Society of Naval Surgeons, though his lectures and the Naval Surgeons' lectures probably took place in the same place in Covent Garden.

19. Hunter's 1752 course consisted of 48 lectures.

20. William Hunter, at the request of Martin Van Butchell, a former pupil of his, who became a well-known dentist, false teeth maker and truss maker, embalmed his wife and she was kept in a glass case in Van Butchell's drawing room. When he remarried he gave his first wife to the Royal College of Surgeons of England, but she was destroyed in the bombing of the College in the Second World War. An account of the actual embalming process is printed in T.J. Pettigrew, *A history of Egyptian Mummies* (London 1834), from papers formerly at the Royal College of Surgeons of England.

21. The last course for which there are notes was in 1781. It ran from September to May and covered lectures on anatomy, surgery, embalming and injecting, with six additional lectures on midwifery.

22. Henry Watson, Reader in Anatomy and surgeon to the Middlesex Hospital, did not attend Hunter's lectures till 1748 (William Hunter, *Medical Commentaries,* vol. I. p.10), so his story cannot relate to Hunter's first four courses of lectures.

23. This story is not substantiated from the dates advertised for the commencement of Hunter's lectures. He gave, in the early years, two courses each year, for which the advertised commencement dates show little variation over six years, except that from 1749 the lectures began earlier in the season (Peachey, *loc. cit.* p.91).

1746	13 October	1746/7	2 February
1747	12 October	1747/8	1 February
1748	10 October	1748/9	23 January
1749	16 September	1749/50	10 January
1750	15 September	1750/51	9 January
1751	13 September	1751/52	5 January

24. Hunter's bank account for 1754-1783, which still survives in the ledgers of Drummond's Branch of the Royal Bank of Scotland, Charing Cross, London, presents a rather different picture of his financial activities. He both lent and possibly borrowed money, played the market buying and selling both government and East India Company stock, and purchasing large numbers of Government Lottery tickets. The foundations of his considerable wealth may well have been a prize in one of the lotteries; unfortunately no prize-lists for the relevant years have survived.

25. It was in 1748, not 1749, that Hunter made his second journey to the continent, for a letter to William Cullen saying 'I had a delightful ride this summer, through Holland and Flanders, on my way to Paris' is dated 20 September, 1748. There is no evidence that on this journey he was accompanied by William George Douglas (Thomson, *loc. cit.* I, p. 539).

26. This type of fracture of the patella had been described by James Douglas, with examples from medical literature, in James Douglas, 'Some remarks upon a transverse Fracture of the Patella', read before the Royal Society 14 November, 1724 (Hunterian Ms. 568).

27. Hoadley, Benjamin, M.D., F.R.S., *Three lectures on the organs of respiration....,* Gulstonian Lectures (London, 1740).
28. Henry Hinckley, King's College, Cambridge. M.D. 1754, Fellow of the Royal College of Physicians 1754, Physician to the Middlesex Hospital 1752, Guy's Hospital 1756, d.1779. His thesis does not appear to have been printed.
29. John Ranby, 1703-1773. Sergeant-Surgeon, Foreign Brother of Barber-Surgeons Company 1722, F.R.S. 1724. Surgeon in Ordinary to George II, on German Campaign and was present at the Battle of Dettingen 1743. The Duke of Cumberland was his patient. Through his interest with the King and the Government he helped to bring about the Separation of the Barbers and Surgeons in 1746, and became first Master of the Surgeons.
30. David Middleton. Senior Surgeon at St. George's Hospital; became Surgeon General to the Army; d.1785.
31. Sir Caesar Hawkins, 1711-1786. Studied medicine with his father and John Ranby. Admitted to the Company of Surgeons, 1735. Surgeon to Prince of Wales, 1737. Surgeon to St. George's Hospital, 1735-1774. Sergeant-Surgeon to George II, 1747; held the same appointment to George III.
32. William Bromfield, 1713-1792. Pupil of John Ranby. A governor of St. George's Hospital; elected a surgeon to the hospital on the resignation of James Wilkie. Surgeon to the Prince and Princess of Wales, and one of the founders of the Lock Hospital, Grosvenor Place, 1746, of which he became First Surgeon. In 1761 he was one of the party sent to Strelitz to attend the Princess of Mecklenburg on her journey to England to marry George III. Appointed Surgeon to Queen Charlotte's household, 1769.
33. John Hunter corrected Simmons's description of Smellie from *coarse* to *large and clumsy.*
34. While Hunter may have treated old patients at the old rate, he was not prepared to accept new patients who could not pay the full fees.

> 'I have known him called out from dinner whilst I was sitting with him, been asked to attend people who did not come up to his price who he has refused with out ever once mentioning me on the occasion.'

(William Hewson's complaint against William Hunter. American Philosophical Society Library, Philadelphia.)
35. '...the same place' refers not to Dr. Douglas's house in Convent Garden, for by now the Douglas household had moved to Hatton Garden, but to the same place as that in which he and the Society of Naval Surgeons had been lecturing.
36. On 11 September, 1761 the following advertisement appeared in the *London Evening Post.*

> Dr. Hunter not having been able to provide himself with convenient appartments thinks it is his duty to inform the students of Anatomy that he is obliged to discontinue his lectures this winter.

From October, 1762 to May, 1763 he lectured in the Chelsea China Warehouse, and from 1763-1767 in a house in Litchfield Street. In October,

1767 he gave his first lectures in Great Windmill Street (Peachey, *loc. cit.* p.112).

37. J. A. Venn, *Alumni Cantabrigiensis,* Part I, vol. IV. 27 (Cambridge, 1927), records Francis Sandys only as a surgeon and lecturer in Anatomy in Cambridge, not as Professor of Anatomy at the university.

38. The date is 1750, not 1751.

39. William Hunter's various purchases of land around Long Calderwood are recorded in the *Records of Sasines,* Register House, Edinburgh. The first purchase was in 1752, for which John Hunter, during his visit to Scotland in 1752, stood witness.

40. In 1734 William Hogarth established the St. Martin's Lane Academy of the Incorporated Society of Artists, at which most of the British artists of the reign of George II and of the early part of the reign of George III received the rudiments of their professional education. The date given by John Hunter (i.e. the early 1750s) for the casting of the muscle man indicates that it was this society that was meant and not the Society of Artists which was not founded till 1760.

Hunter subscribed to Hogarth's *Analysis of Beauty* (1752) (G.U. Hunter Papers H247c) and to a print of an Election Entertainment (G.U. Hunter Papers H247d) and may have met Hogarth through Bernard Baron who worked for James Douglas, and later engraved for Hogarth.

A life-size plaster cast of a muscle man, said to have been made by William Hunter, is still available to students in the Life School at the Royal Academy of Arts, London [Plate V], though it is not the same one as that shown in J. Zoffany's Dr. William Hunter lecturing at the Royal Academy of Arts [Plate VII]. Besides this early cast, Hunter is known to have been responsible for two others, one of a Jew executed for robbery 1771, the making of which is recorded in William W. Whitley's *Artists and their friends,* 1707-1799, vol.I, p.277, and another which is still in the Royal Academy, known as 'Smugglerius': it is of a smuggler posed as the Dying Gladiator *(ibid.* vol. II, p.285-6) [Plate IX]. A small wax ecorché of a muscle man, made by Edward Birch [Plate X], similar to the life size plaster cast in Zoffany's picture, is in the Hunterian Museum, Glasgow, and other examples are known. Hunter, through George III, was appointed Professor of Anatomy at the Royal Academy at its founding in 1768. Till this story of John's it was not known that William had had previous experience in lecturing to artists. See also Martin Kemp, *Dr. William Hunter at the Royal Academy of Arts* (Glasgow, 1975).

41. Glasgow University awarded William Hunter the M.D. degree on 2nd October, 1750. W. Innes Anderson, *A Roll of the Graduates of the University of Glasgow* (Glasgow, 1898).

That same year, 1 August, the City of Edinburgh made him a Burgess and Guild Brother (Hunter-Baillie Papers 6, f.20). In 1751 he became an Honorary Member of the Faculty of Physicians and Surgeons, Glasgow (A. Duncan, *Memorial of the Faculty of Physicians and Surgeons of Glasgow,* Glasgow, 1896). It was not till 1761 that he was admitted a Burgess of Glasgow (Hunter-Baillie Papers 6, f.7).

42. At the Court of Assistants of the Surgeon's Company, held 1 July, 1756,

It having been reported to the Court that Dr. William Hunter, a member of this Company was desirous of being disfranchised on such terms as the Court should agree, it was ordered that the clerk so deliver him the instrument of disfranchisement under the Seal of the Company on his paying down forty guineas for the same, being the same terms as were granted to Dr. Wathen on 6 December, 1753.

(Minutes of the Court of Assistants of the Corporation of Surgeons, quoted from Peachey.)

Hunter was admitted a Licentiate of the Royal College of Physicians on 30 September, 1756. However, he had neglected to obtain, as he should have done, permission from the Corporation of Surgeons to become a Licentiate of the Royal College of Physicians, for it is recorded,

> Mr. Sainthill having received £20 from Dr. Hunter, being the penalty he had incurred by becoming a member of the College of Physicians without previous consent of this Court, a motion was made and seconded that as leave had been granted to Dr. Kelly and Dr. Hunter was ignorant of the by-law the fine now paid on his behalf should be returned to Mr. Sainthill in order to be given back by him to the Doctor, and the question being put it was carried in the affirmative.

(Minutes of the Court of Assistants of the Corporation of Surgeons.)

It is therefore difficult to understand John Hunter's remark. It may have been that he was thinking of the time between William becoming an M.D. – 1750 – when he would have been entitled to call himself Doctor and seek a licence from the Royal College of Physicians, and 1756, when he actually took this step.

43. The Society of Hospital Physicians, sometimes called the Medical Society, that published *Medical Observations and Inquiries.*

44. The controversy with John Douglas (not the brother of James Douglas) centred on who had first described a true aneurism as due only to a dilatation of the artery. This Hunter credited to Paulus Aegineta. John Douglas, who reviewed Hunter's paper in the *Monthly Review* (vol. 16, 1757, p. 541) claimed it was Galen who first described a true aneurism and accused Hunter of ignorance of the works of Latin medical writers. The *Critical Review* (vol. 4, 1757, p.35), in the person of Tobias Smollett, supported Hunter's interpretation and, in turn, accused Douglas of ignorance in his failure to understand Galen. Douglas retaliated with *A letter to the author of the Critical Review* (London, 1757), provoking a reply in the *Critical Review* (vol. 17, p.279), after which the controversy ended, for Douglas died soon after.

45. William Hunter, 'Further observations upon a particular species of Aneurism', *Medical Observations and Inquiries,* 2 (1762) 390-414.
A letter from Mr. Thomas Armiger, Surgeon, to William Hunter, M.D., F.R.S. On the varicose aneurism, *Medical Observations and Inquiries,* 4 (1771), 337-384.
William Hunter, 'A postscript to the preceeding case of the varicose aneurism', *Medical Observations and Inquiries,* 4 (1771) 385-387.

46. William Hunter, 'The history of an emphysema', *Medical Observations and Inquiries,* 2 (1762), 17-69.

47. William Hunter, 'An account of a diseased tibia', *Medical Observations and Inquiries*, 2 (1762), 303-306.
48. William Hunter, 'Remarks on the Symphysis of the ossa pubis', *Medical Observations and Inquiries*, 2 (1762), 333-339.
49. John Tickel, Surgeon, 'Observations on the insensibility of tendons', with an introduction by Dr. Hunter, *Medical Observations and Inquiries*, 4 (1771) 343-346.
50. William Hunter, 'An appendix to the history of a Fatal inversion of the uterus by Mr. John Lynn', *Medical Observations and Inquiries*, 4 (1771) 400-409. William Hunter, 'Summary remarks on the retroverted uterus', *Medical Observations and Inquiries*, 5 (1776) 388-393.
51. William Hunter, 'On the uncertainty of the signs of murder in the case of bastard children', *Medical Observations*, 6 (1784) 266-290. William Hunter, 'Three cases of mal-formation of the heart', *ibid.*, 291-309. William Hunter, 'The successful cure of a severe disorder of the stomach by milk taken in small quantities at once', *ibid.*, 310-318.
52. It has been suggested that' William Hunter gave no lectures between September, 1761 and September, 1762 mainly because he was in attendance upon Queen Charlotte for the birth of her first child.
53. Letter from students to William Hunter:

Sir.

The Singular Benifits we have deriv'd from this Course of Lectures: The Pains you have taken to qualifie us for an advantageous Prosecution of our Studies; & ye concern you have manifested for ye wellfare of your Pupils: demand our utmost Thanks.

The notice we receiv'd of your Intention to decline reading as soon as you finished the first Course, gave a Damp to all our wishes, & check'd the ardor of our Pursuits, but when we reflected on ye high Rank you hold in Anatomy, the great applause you have so justly acquired in teaching & your willingness to promote this important Study, we could not but look upon you as the Patron of this Science; & a Consideration of ye irreparable Loss we must have sustain'd should you intermit Lectures at so critical Juncture, gave us Room to hope you might be prevail'd upon, by our Petition to fav' us with a second Course.

Nor did our Hopes prove abortive; on the contrary, our most sanguine Expectations were answered, & our highest ambition fully gratify'd. – The constant Fatigue of an established & extensive Practice amongst Persons of the first Distinction could not prevent an opportunity of indulging a benevolent Disposition, by complying with our Requests. Your many important Avocations only serv'd as Circumstances to enhance ye Obligations; and the generous manner of conferring it gave us the highest susceptibility of Pleasure and Gratitude.

We have it not in our Power to make any satisfaction adequate to the Merit, or deep sense we shall ever retain of this mark of your Favr, but we should be greatly wanting to ourselves, did we not improve this occasion of expressing our acknowledgements for this indutable Instance of your Goodness, wch deserves to be had in lasting Remembrance. – Such a generous Action has acquired our greatful Esteem, the highest respect for your distinguish'd Character; & the most warm and affectionate wishes for your continued welfare.

London. March 18. 1761   By order of the Class.
To Dr. Wm. Hunter.

At the foot of the letter, in Hunter's handwriting, the name, 'John Morgan'. Morgan, one of his pupils, was an American from Philadelphia. He was, with William Shippen, another of Hunter's pupils, the founder of the first medical school in America at Philadelphia (Hunter Papers, H 43).

A further letter, of which the original has now been lost but which is printed in Prof. John Young's tribute to William Hunter in *Record of the Ninth Jubilee of the University of Glasgow* (Glasgow, 1901), pp.105-6, refers to the proposed silver cup to be made by Mr. Crisp:

Sir,
We are now just entering into the World, are at a time of life which must determine our future Characters and Success in it. We have ambitions as become us, and our title to Fame is by no means ill-founded, having been your Pupils, if of such an advantage we have made a proper use.

Desirous, then, of appearing Men of Consequence, yet conscious of our inability to rise on Merit all our own, we count the World's applause as Patrons of Ingenuity, and are attempting to build our Fame on a surer Foundation – by setting forth the Merit of Others. A Device this which we hope will meet with your Approbation and Countenance.

With this View, permit us to presume so much on your friendly Disposition as to introduce to your knowledge Mr. Crisp, the Nature of whose visit will be better explained to you by himself than we can do it in writing. He will, by our Order, present to you one of his Performances, and if it should so far meet with your Approbation as to be honoured with a place on your Sideboard, he will at least have good Reason to believe himself safe from the awkward Censure of pretended Judges; whilst we shall have a certain praiseworthy Pleasure in having communicated to Posterity the Fame of a distinguished Character, Countenanced by your Authority. Our Patronage must have its Weight, as Numbers will crowd in to your Opinion and think it thus honourable to agree in Sentiments with Dr. Hunter.

Here were it not for offending only you Sir, we might give, in drawing your Character, the fullest liberty to our Pen, without any Danger of being deemed Flatterers; but Cautious to avoid every Danger of offending whilst our Ambition is to live in your Memory we curb even the Dictates of a grateful Heart. Think not, however, that We are Insensible of the many Obligations which you have conferred on Us, but do us the Honour to believe that it will be the anxious Endeavour of all of us to have deserved them: and permit us with all Respect, and with every good wish for your Health and Happiness, to subscribe ourselves, Sir, your much obliged and very humble servants.

(Signed by his pupils)

54. Percivall Pott, *A treatise on ruptures.* The second edition, altered, corrected and improved (London, 1763).

55. William Hunter, *A supplement to the first part of Medical Commentaries* (London, 1764).

56. A set of notes of Hunter's 1752 Anatomy Lectures, taken by Charles White, recently discovered in Australia and now published, *William Hunter's Lectures of Anatomy* (Amsterdam, 1972), proves that Hunter had, in his lectures, described the lymphatic system as the absorbent system of the body before Alexander Monro, Secundus, claimed to have discovered this.

57. Hunter claimed he received the first hint of the lymphatics being absorbent vessels from 'a friend asking his opinion of Mr. Freke's Chirurgical Publications in the year 1748, which he had not [then] read. Mr. Freke advising a surgeon in venereal cases to cut out a bubo from the groin, for he said he would by that means eradicate the poison which he supposed was conveyed in some way or other to the inguinal gland'. Royal College of Surgeons of England, Ms. 42. d. 11. Notes of Lectures by William Hunter and William Cruickshank. John Freke, *An essay on the art of healing* (London, 1748).

58. William Hunter, *Medical Commentaries,* Part 1 (London, 1762), p.75-89.

59. In 1753 William Hunter, with Percival Pott, was elected a Master of Anatomy at Surgeon's Hall. Peachey and others have assumed that it was John Hunter who was elected, but the By-laws of the Company of Surgeons required the Masters of Anatomy to be elected from members of the Company. In 1753 William was a member, John was not.

60. It is plain, from William Hunter's *Anatomy of the human gravid uterus* (Birmingham, 1744) that William Hunter had, by 1751, established all that John had claimed. But neither John nor William could rightly claim that they had proved that though maternal blood passed into the placenta there is no direct connection between the blood systems of the mother and the foetus. This had been demonstrated by injection in 1743 by W. Noortwyk, though he did not care to conclude this was so from his injections. His findings had been confirmed by Albinus in 1748. Hunter saw the preparations of both these men when he visited Holland in 1748 *(Medical Commentaries* (1762) Part I p.52).

61. The second child, and first son, of George III's eldest sister, the Hereditary Princess (later Duchess) of Brunswick-Wolfenbüttel, was born during a visit of his parents to England. But this was not till 8 February, 1766. Since it was in 1762 that William Hunter had first attended Queen Charlotte, and the same year, not 1764 as stated by Simmons, had been appointed her Physician in Extraordinary, it is more likely that it was the Queen who recommended William Hunter to the Duchess of Brunswick. (Personal communication from Miss Olwen Hedley.)

62. A transcript of William Hewson's account of the controversy is in the Library of the American Philosophical Society, Philadelphia, Pennsylvania. William Hunter's account is in Lloyd G. Stevenson, 'William Hewson, the Hunters and Benjamin Franklin', *J. Hist. Med.,* 8 (1953), 324-328.

63. Sir John Pringle (1707-1782). See Dictionary of National Biography. He was a friend of William Hunter.

64. Mary Hewson, daughter of Mrs. Stevenson, Benjamin Franklin's landlady in London. Franklin was also a friend of William Hunter and attempted to mediate between Hunter and Hewson. (Letter from Franklin to Hunter, Hunter-Baillie Papers Vol. 1, f.36.) After Hewson's death, his wife, on encouragement from Franklin, emigrated to Philadelphia.

65. See Kemp, *William Hunter at the Royal Academy of Art* (Glasgow, 1975).

66. The Society of Collegiate Physicians.

67. William Hunter, *Supplement to the first part of Medical Commentaries* (London, 1764).

68. The plaster-casts are in the Anatomy Museum, Glasgow University.

69. James Douglas, William Hunter's teacher, left a large collection of drawings of the gravid uterus and of the foetus *in utero* with descriptions of the drawings. All these drawings came into William Hunter's possession.

70. See J. L. Thornton and Patricia C. Want, 'Artist versus engraver in William Hunter's Anatomy of the human gravid uterus', *Med. Biol. Illust.,* 24 (1974), 137-139.

71. The drawings relating to early embryos and the conception in the Fallopian tube do not now exist. Matthew Baillie published *An anatomical description of the human gravid uterus* by the late Dr. William Hunter (London, 1794). In the introduction he mentions that Hunter's manuscript was not quite complete, and that he has attempted to complete it. In completing the work he describes the decidua as formed from coagulable lymph, a description that John Hunter gave to it, whereas William Hunter initially described it as formed from the inner lining of the uterus. However, William Hunter in his 1781 lectures (Royal College of Surgeons. Ms. 42. a.31) himself described the decidua as formed from coagulable lymph. Before this is considered as a retrograde step, it is necessary to consider both what coagulable lymph was held to be and the part it was thought to play in growth.

> The coagulation of blood, when out of circulation, would seem unconnected with life, yet life could not go on without it; for all the solid parts of the body are formed from the blood; and this could not take place if there did not exist in it the power of coagulation. John Hunter, *A treatise on the blood, inflammation and gun-shot wounds* (London, 1794).

72. John Hunter, *The natural history of the human teeth* (London, 1771).

73. No manuscript on urinary and biliary concretions can now be found. There are three volumes of figures of calculi, the majority drawn by J. V. Rymskyk, and many of these drawings were engraved mainly by Thomas Donaldson. (Hunterian Mss. 69, 70, 71.) A few of the specimens from which the drawings were made are amongst the Hunterian pathological specimens at the Royal Infirmary, Glasgow. In the catalogue of Hunter's Anatomical

Preparations, prepared by Hunter's Trustees, the section listing specimens of calculi contains also a general account of the different types (Hunterian Ms. 638).

74. These were published posthumously as W. Hunter, *Two Introductory lectures.... To which are added some papers relating to Dr. Hunter's intended plan, for the improvement of anatomy, surgery and physic* (London, 1784). The original manuscript for the two introductory lectures turned up in a sale at Sotheby's in 1977. It was acquired by Mr. Jeremy Norman, California, a dealer in rare medical works. While the work was published as the introduction to his last course of lectures, the manuscript was titled as introductory lectures to his first course in his new lecture theatre in Great Windmill St., 1767.

75. No collection of 'cases of dissection' now exists.

76. W. Hunter, *Of the Origin of the Lues venerea,* Read 14 December, 1775 (Royal Society L. & P. VI. 15). In addition to a copy of the paper to the Royal Society, there is amongst the Hunter Papers a collection of letters relating to Hunter's work on this subject, including the draft of a letter to David Hume in Paris, 16 August, 1764, containing a statement of Hunter's opinions on the subject, with a request that Hume would show it to Dr. Astruc, and begging them both to get, if they could, certain information from Salamanca. There is a reply in French addressed to Hume, giving some of the information requested. David Hume's reply to William Hunter is in the Hunter-Baillie Papers, Vol. 1. f.49. Hunter obtained further information from the Count de Viry. (Hunter Papers H 117-121.)

77. W. Hunter, *Reflections occasioned by the Decree of the Faculty of Medicine at Paris upon the operation of cutting the symphysis of the ossa pubis.* Published as an appendix to G. Vaughan, *Cases and observations on Hydrophobia etc.,* 2nd edition (London, 1778).

78. See William Hunter, *Two introductory lectures....*(1784).

79. See Samuel Johnson, *Letters,* vol. II, p.437, edited by G. Birkbeck Hill (Oxford, 1892) in which it is claimed that Samuel Johnson suggested to Hunter that he left his collections to Glasgow University.

80. William Hunter gave his first lectures at Great Windmill St. in 1767 and moved there to live in 1768, when he made over the lease of his Jermyn St. house to John Hunter.

81. He had been collecting books for many years. Writing to William Cullen, 3 August, 1754,

> What say you to Mead's auction of books? I am afraid I shall ruin myself in the winter with it. (Thomson 1. p.546.)

He also bought pictures and antiques at Mead's sale.

82. There were in all four editions of Edward Harwood's *View of the various editions of the Greek and Roman Classics* (London, 1775, 1778, 1782 and 1790). In none of the three later editions have the references to Dr. Hunter, which occur in the first edition, been eliminated.

83. From William Hunter's account with Drummond's Bank, now Drummond's Branch. Royal Bank of Scotland, Charing Cross, London. Hunter paid £1,000 for John Fothergill's shells.

84. See Peter Clare, *A new and easy method of curing the lues venerea* (London, 1780), p. XX.
85. Dr. Baillie, Professor of Divinity at Glasgow University, husband of William Hunter's sister, Dorothy, and father of Matthew Baillie.
86. This almost certainly refers to the same projected purchase of an estate as mentioned by John Hunter on page 24.
87. £8,000 was left to the Professors of Glasgow University,

> representing the said University and to be applied by them... towards purchasing a spot or piece of Ground in or near the College of Glasgow & towards erecting and building thereon a fit and commodious house or Building for the reception of my books and all the....articles contained in my museum.

(Dr. Hunter's Scottish Will. Scottish Record Office, Edinburgh.)
88. By his Scottish Will, William Hunter, who thought that he was legally entitled to leave it to whom he liked, left all his property in Scotland, including Long Calderwood, to Matthew Baillie (Deposition of William Hunter's Scottish Will, Scottish Record Office, Edinburgh). Matthew Baillie instructed Robert Barclay, solicitor, of Capelrig, to draw up deeds transferring Long Calderwood to John Hunter (Hunter-Baillie Papers). However, Barclay found that, legally, Long Calderwood should have gone to John Hunter (Hunter-Baillie Papers, Hunterian Society at the Wellcome Library of the History of Medicine).
89. Johann Zoffany's *Dr. William Hunter lecturing at the Royal Academy of Arts.* This appears to have been a copy of a nearly completed picture by Zoffany which was bought by Matthew Baillie in 1814 from Mr. Damerque who had bought it at Mr. Doratt's Sale. This picture he afterwards gave to the College of Physicians. Mr Doratt was son-in-law of Zoffany, and a doctor. The unfinished copy has disappeared. Zoffany painted another picture in which William Hunter figures, *The life school at the Royal Academy of Arts,* now in the possession of Her Majesty the Queen [Plate XI].
90. The original portrait by Chamberlin is at the Royal Academy of Arts [Plate VIII].
91. William Hunter was noted for his plain living,

> When he invited his younger friends to table, they were seldom regaled with more than two dishes; when alone, he rarely sat down to more than one: he would say *"A man who cannot live on this, deserves to have no dinner."*

(W. McMichael, *Lives of the British Physicians,* London, 1830.)
and
Letter from William Hunter to Dr. Cumming, December 7, 1781.

> I have only to thank you for a thousand kindnesses and scold you for sending a Hare for one who neither eats himself, nor has ever anybody to eat with him except they prefer cheese or cowheel to game.

(Copy in the Pultney Correspondence, Linnaean Society, London.)
92. W. Hunter, 'Reflections on dividing the Symphysis pubis', Supplement to J. Vaughan, *Observations on the hydrophobia etc.* (London, 1778).

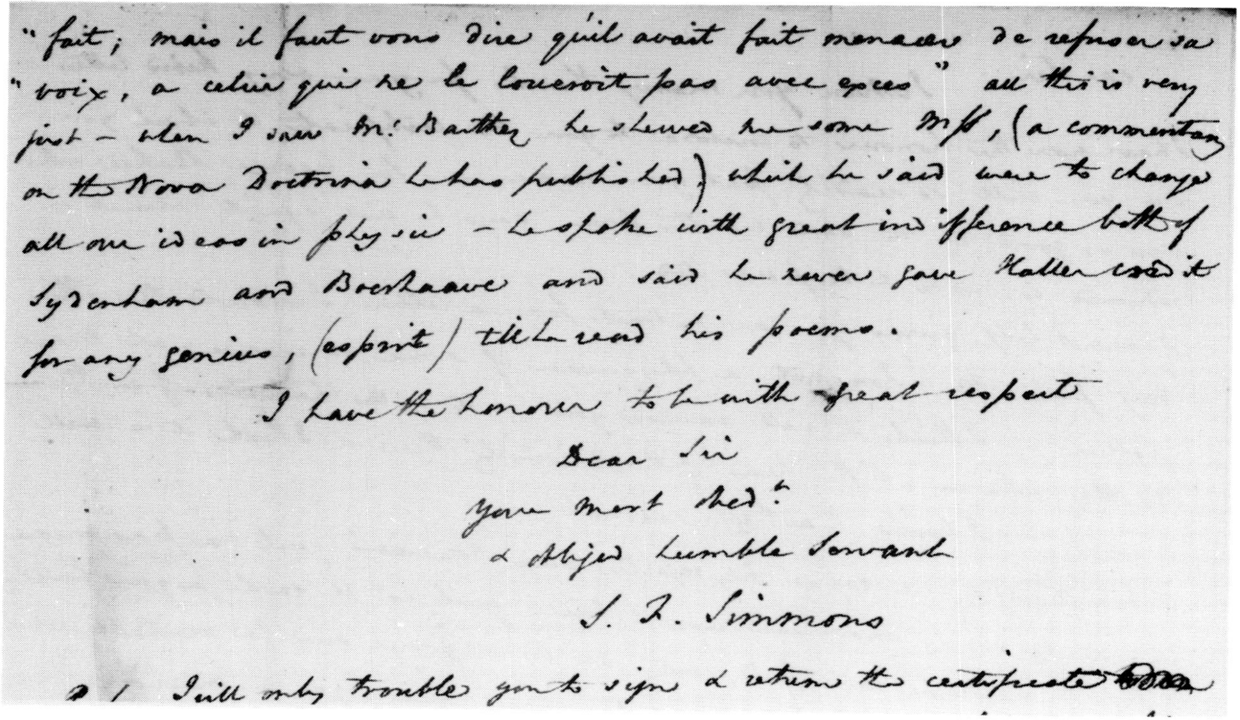

Plate II Part of letter from Samuel Foart Simmons to William Cullen. Thomson/Cullen Papers, University of Glasgow Library

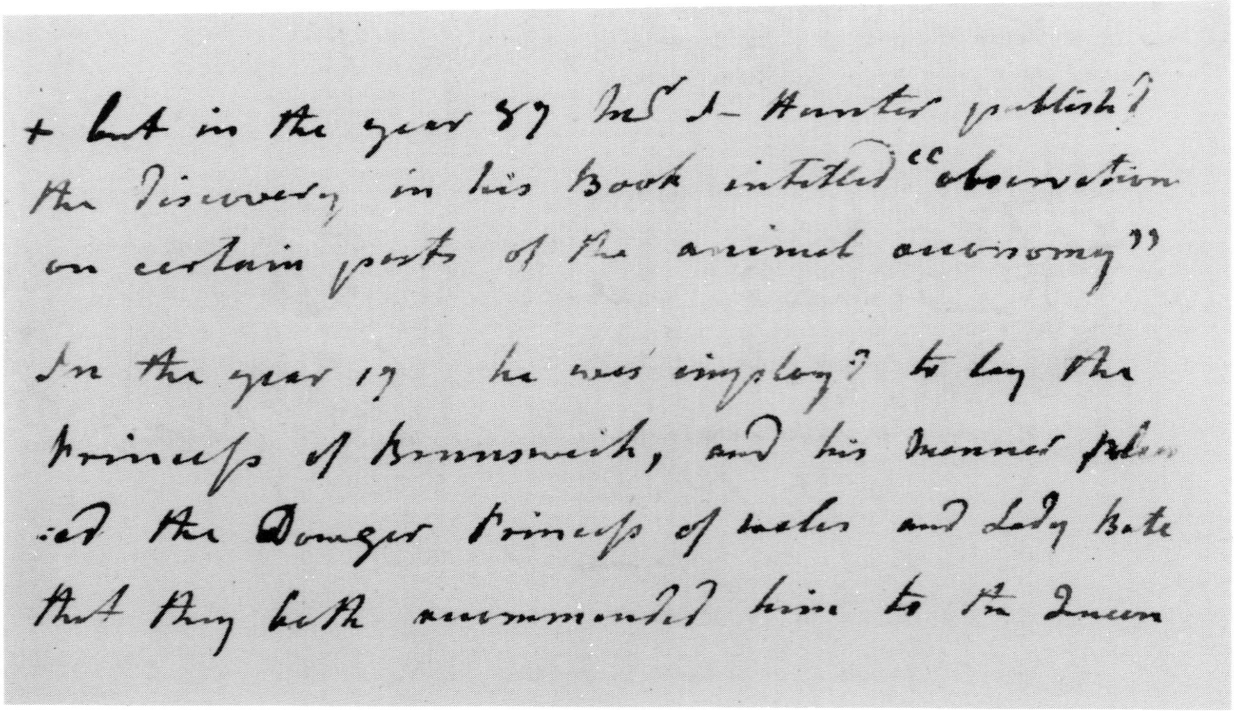
+ but in the year 87 Mr J. Hunter publish'd
the Discovery in his Book intitled "observation
on certain parts of the animal oeconomy"

In the year 17 he was employ'd to lay the
Princess of Brunswick, and his manner plea-
:sed the Dowager Princess of wales and Lady Bute
that they both recommended him to the Queen

Plate III Note in interleaved copy of Samuel Foart Simmons's *Life of Dr. William Hunter*, University of Glasgow Library

Dear Jenner

I recd yours and was extremely happy to hear of your Success in business, I hope it will continue. I am oblig'd to you for thinking of me especially in my natural History. I shall be glad of your observations on the Cuckow and upon the breeding of Toads, be as particular as you possibly can; If you can pick me up any thing that is curious, and prepare it for me. Do it, either in the Flesh or Fish way. Pictures have been very cheap, but the Season is now over. There will be but one Sale, viz Jordyens but I believe that all his Pictures are capital and will go beyond you or me. Since you wrote to me I pickd up a Small Landscape of Berchetts of Cattle and Herd. I give 5:7:6.

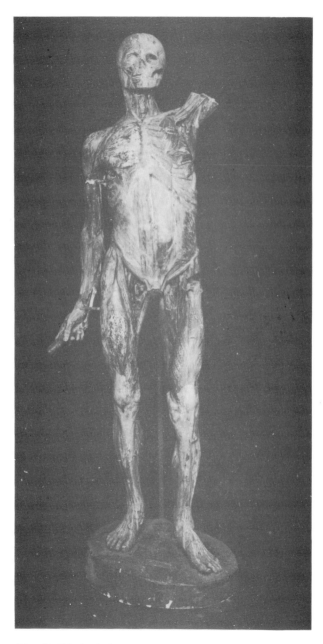

Plate V Life-sized plaster cast of muscle man said to have been made by William Hunter. Royal Academy of Arts, London

Plate VI   Dr. Hunter's silver cup. Hunterian Museum, University of Glasgow

Plate VII   Johann Zoffany. William Hunter lecturing at the Royal Academy of Arts. Royal College of Physicians, London

Plate VIII   Mason Chamberlin. William Hunter.
Royal Academy of Arts, London

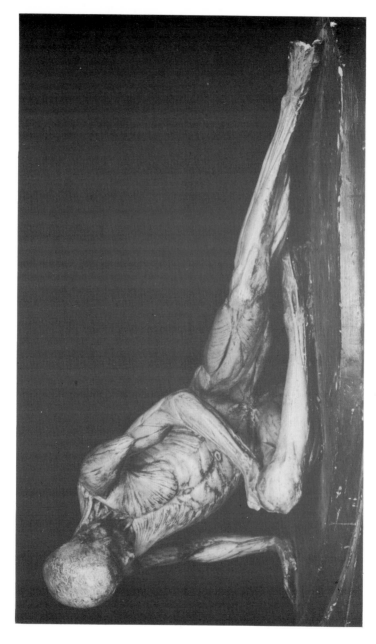

Plate IX Life-sized plaster cast of muscle man posed as the Dying Gladiator and known as Smugglerius, said to have been made by William Hunter. Royal Academy of Arts, London

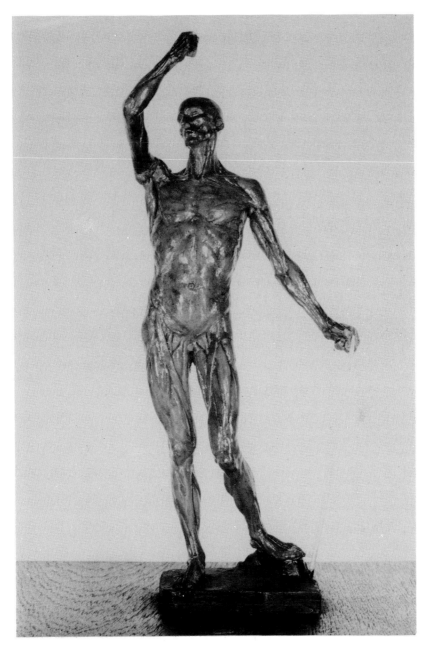

Plate X   Wax écorché made by Edward Burch. Hunterian Museum, University of Glasgow

Plate XI Johann Zoffany. The life school at the Royal Academy. Her Majesty the Queen

Plate XII   The Anatomist overtaken by the Watch

Plate XIII The Resurrection

WILLIAM HUNTER

A Reassessment

S IMMONS'S *Life and writings of the late William Hunter* has been reprinted
because it is a valuable source, made even more valuable by John Hunter's
additons. But it is not a balanced assessment of William Hunter. This reassessment is an attempt to remedy some of this imbalance and to use some of
the material that is now available about him.

Simmons did not contact the one person who could have given him
information about William's boyhood, his sister Dorothy, only two and a half
years younger. She described him as 'a steady friend and affectionate brother' but
added that as a boy he was

> of a diligent and careful disposition, indefatigable in making himself
> master of anything he wished to know, but at the same time having a
> relish for anything drole or characteristic, and taking a great
> pleasure in conversing with the country people and amusing
> himself with their peculiarities, which he had a peculiar turn for
> drawing out. He was of principles to be depended upon at all times
> for doing right, and ready to lift up his hand in defense of his
> brothers and sisters, but not of that frank and open disposition
> which makes those of less steady principles and weaker affections
> more beloved'.[1]

Certainly, as William's fortunes rose, he gave financial assistance to members
of the family. 'I shall always think it the happiness of Riches to support
Relations'.[2] But in the correspondence between brother and sister there is little
warmth and Dorothy's letters to her brother always appear constrained as if she
were determined to avoid any grounds for offence.

The one surviving letter to William from his father records the disappointment
of an old man that William was planning his life without any regard for his
family.[3] The one known letter from William to his mother[4] showed that he had
neglected to write to her for three months after James Douglas's death, till she
had heard of it from another source and had worried over the future prospects of
both William and his brother, James, who had joined him in the Douglas
household. She was to continue to complain about the infrequency of his letters.[5]

William Cullen seems to have been mainly responsible for keeping William in touch with his family at Long Calderwood. In 1751, when Cullen wrote to him to tell him that his mother was dying of cancer of the stomach and longed to see her favourite son, John, then working in London with William, he replied:

> I cannot consent this season to her request, for my brother's sake, for my own sake and even for my mother's sake. It would be every way a bad scheme. I have wrote of it to her and hope she will consider better of it and find that it is really a whim begot of sickness and low spirits.[6]

Though William had been back at Long Calderwood the previous year, could he have been motivated by jealousy that it was John only that his mother wished to see? Cullen commented sadly:

> She says nothing now about Johnies' coming down, but I know in her present temper it would have pleased her much if he had.[7]

Mrs. Hunter died in November of that year. Dorothy, now left alone, was taken into the Cullen household till John, who now could be spared by William, the following summer was sent to bring her back to London to live with William till her marriage to Dr. James Buchanan in 1758.

Between William and his elder brother, James, there was a close friendship, and from the correspondence between them there emerges the clearest picture of William as a young man in London. Writing the night before he left for France in 1743 with William George Douglas, William tells of his hopes of establishing himself in his 'darling London'. He comments on the attitude of the Douglas family to him

> The kindness I have met with in this family is infinitely more than I deserve and a good deal more than I expected....I need not mention particulars but everything will be to my wish.

This has been taken to imply that he was engaged to be married to James Douglas's daughter, Martha Jane. London life and his entry into medical practice required him to be suitably clothed, an expense that he could ill afford.

> I have cleared off Paton and every other creditor of yours or mine except the Taylor (which has cost me the matter of 17 pounds) and him I have given a note of hand for the remainder of what I owe him.[8]

But he never 'suffered his economy to interfere where the dignity.... of his character' was concerned.

While he was in Paris Martha Jane died, but Hunter returned to the Douglas household and managed to write cheerfully to James:

> Our friend Oswald had a Benefit Concert the other day where I was present. I need not say I was agreeably entertained, for you know I love music; but when I say I was perfectly happie you must suspect that there was more than meere sound in the case.

Possibly another love affair was developing.

It was not only concerts that he patronised, for his letter continued:

> Thursday I went to see Mr Thomson's Tancrede and Sigismunde. It
> was the third night, the Authors. Here again I was happy enough, &
> chiefly for the same reason.[9]

Then he gives a long criticism of the play and the production, and promises to
send James a copy of it when it was published. Whether James ever got the letter,
written 23 March, 1745, is doubtful, and almost certainly he never got the play,
for by 11 April he died from consumption, which had probably been responsible
already for carrying off five of his brothers and sisters.

*   *   *   *   *   *   *

In spite of all that has been written, no satisfactory account of the changing
relationship between William and his brother John has ever been given. When
John joined William in London in 1748 they must have been virtual strangers to
each other, having been separated for eight years, during which John had grown
from adolescence to young manhood. Though temperamentally very different,
the first ten years of their association appears to have passed smoothly. But
John's health began to suffer[10] from long hours of work dissecting, and from
living in London. It has been suggested that it was as an escape from London and
anatomy that he was sent, in 1752, to Scotland to bring Dorothea back to live with
William; and it was arranged, for the same reason, in 1755 for him to enter St.
Mary's Hall, Oxford, as a Gentleman Commoner, though he stayed there less
than a year. In 1760, again probably because his health was giving trouble, he
joined the army as a surgeon and was sent to Portugal. His letters to William from
Portugal were always friendly, and he invariably signed himself 'Your affectionate
brother'.

In 1763, after peace was declared, John left the army and returned to London,
but not to work with William. He decided to make his own way in the profession.
A dispute then developed as to the ownership of the anatomical preparations
made by John while he was working with William. John must have pressed his
claim to them somewhat freely and forcibly against William's belief that they
were his property, for Tobias Smollett, a friend of both, appended to a letter to
William on 14 June, 1763:

> I cannot help expressing an eager Desire that your Brother's future
> conduct may intitle him to a revival of more favorable sentiments in
> you which he has indiscreetly forfeited.[11]

Though the brothers had separated and quarrelled, and the cause of the
quarrel was to influence the contract of partnership William entered into with
William Hewson,[12] who took John's place, a friendly relationship was re-
established between the brothers. They consulted together and helped each
other at operations and post-mortems. John, with only his army half-pay as
regular income, as yet little private practice and no hospital appointment, must
often have been short of money, and William made, during the years up to John's
marriage, a series of payments to him,[13] whether for dissections, for specimens
obtained for the museum or just to help him out is not recorded.

Another suggested cause of friction was William's supposed jealousy of John,
elected a Fellow of the Royal Society in 1767, three months before William was

elected.[14] At this date, John had published nothing though he had, in 1766, given a paper to the Society on the mud iguana *(Siren lacertina).* William had two papers in the *Philosophical Transactions,* several important papers in *Medical Observations and Inquiries,* as well as having published *Medical Commentaries,* though this work may have done more to enhance John's reputation than his own. John had no public appointment while William was Physician in Extraordinary to Queen Charlotte, and had a number of influential friends. Moreover, not only had John been educated in anatomy and techniques of dissection and injection by William, but his early work had been undertaken under William's direction in aspects of anatomy which were primarily of interest to William. Short of time to do the work himself, William supplied the stimulus, John reacted with great success through his mastery of the necessary skills. Though by 1767 John had demonstrated his independent inspiration and skill in attacking biological problems, one can imagine that William may have felt aggrieved at the pupil being honoured before the teacher. But if he did, there was at that time no public display of hostility between the two.

In 1768 John was appointed surgeon at St. George's Hospital, where William may well have used his influence and canvassed Lord Hertford and Garrick, governors of the hospital, on his behalf. When William, in 1768, moved into his new house in Great Windmill Street, John took over the lease of the house in Jermyn Street.

John's marriage to Ann Home in 1771 has sometimes been made the grounds for a quarrel between the brothers. John, writing to William to announce his intended marriage:

> Dear Brother.
> Tomorrow at eight oclock and at St. James's Church I enter into the Holy State of Matrimony. As that is a ceremony which you are not particularly fond of, I will not make a point of having your company there. I propose going out of town for a few days; when I come to Town I shall call upon you.
> Married or not, ever yours
> > John Hunter.[15]

Even if William disapproved of John's marriage, or of marriage in general, they still continued to work together, and when John was taken seriously ill in 1773, William was one of the doctors who attended him. But there were hints of gathering tension; Horace Walpole, a friend of both the Hunters, writing to Lady Ossory, one of William's patients, in 1776, remarked

> The quarrel between SS. Cosmo and Damian they say is at an end.[16]

St. Cosmas and St. Damian, twin brothers and doctors, are, with St. Luke, the patron saints of physicians and surgeons, and the remark is said to relate to William and John Hunter.

Jesse Foot, in his biased biography of John, suggests another quarrel over an anatomical preparation:

> John Hunter having invited William to the sight of a diseased part of a soldier who had died in consequence of it:– and William having

found that this diseased anatomical property, would form a valuable preparation for his museum, caused it to be taken to his house and refused to give it up to the claim made by John. This was resented by John, and this proved to be so serious a foundation, for the separation of friendship and affection between the two brothers as never afterwards found any abatement.[17]

Whether or not there is truth in this story, John, in 1780, in what looks like an attack on William, read a paper to the Royal Society in which he claimed that it was he who had first explained

> the structure of the human placenta and its connection with the uterus, together with the use arising from such structure and communication and having first demonstrated the vascularity of the spongy chorion.[18]

He based this claim on a dissection he had carried out with Dr. Colin Mackenzie in 1754.

It was John's claim that he was the first to demonstrate that maternal blood passed into sinuses in the placenta, into which the capillaries of the umbilical vessels dipped and absorbed nutrients for the foetus from the maternal blood but that there was no direct connection between the blood system of the mother and foetus. This was an observation that neither John nor William could claim, having been demonstrated, but not clearly understood by William Noortwyk in 1743[19] and later confirmed by Albinus in 1746.[20] William had seen Noortwyk's preparations[21] and probably those of Albinus as well when he visited Holland in 1748. William had confirmed these observations for himself in 1750 in a dissection in which, almost certainly, John assisted.

Initially, William had some difficulty in interpreting the observations, because it was generally supposed that a layer of foetal tissue, the spongy chorion, separated the placenta from the uterus, so that the placenta was looked on as a wholly foetal production. But when, as William recorded:

> My brother and I have more than once observed that beginning at the edge of the os tincae to separate the spongey chorion from the inside of the uterus we find that upon that part of the ovum opposite the os tincae where there is of course no internal surface of the uterus opposed at that spot there is no spongey chorion Which is a strong presumption that it is only generated by the internal surface of the uterus.[22]

It was obvious that no foetal material separated the placenta from the uterus. William was then able to describe, as he did in a letter to Albrecht von Haller in 1765,[23] the placenta as a composite structure formed partly from foetal, partly from maternal material, and the vascular nature of the spongey chorion, supplied by vessels from the uterine wall from which it was formed. This description has stood the test of time. Because the spongey chorion came away at birth he called it the *decidua*. He thought that at the edge of the placenta part of the decidua, which he called the *decidua reflexa,* was reflected up over the embryo, the rest of the *decidua,* that lining the general cavity of the uterus and lying between the uterus and placenta, he called the *decidua vera.* As the embryo grows, the *decidua reflexa* becomes pressed against the *decidua vera* and forms with it a single membrane. He was not in a position to know that this duplicature of the decidua resulted not from the membrane growing over the embryo but from the embryo becoming embedded in the uterine wall.

After John's paper, William wrote to the Secretary of the Royal Society, asking him to read to the Society a letter[24] in which he pointed out that it was he, not John, who had explained the relationship between the mother and foetus *in utero,* and asking the Secretary to obtain from John 'the grounds for Mr. Hunter's claim'. His letter was duly read to the Society at the next meeting. John's reply to the enquiry merely reiterated his former claim and asked for William to produce evidence 'of his having discovered this anatomical fact at any period of time prior to this conference with Dr. Mackenzie'.[25] This, in its turn, was read to the Society. There, apparently, the argument rested. The Royal Society did not publish John's paper in the *Philosophical Transactions.* It was not till 1786 that John published his account of the argument, [26] not exactly in the form it had been given to the Royal Society, and when William could no longer, in print, refute John's claim. Yet, confirmation of William's position is in his *Anatomy of the human gravid uterus,* plate X, and its description, dating from 1751, in which all John's claims are described and illustrated. It is a measure of the failure of William's magnificent production to be considered as more than a collection of fine engravings of magnificent anatomical drawings that it was not used, nor has it since been used effectively, to refute John's attack. Moreover, William in this publication gives generous praise to John for his help with the work.

After this there was, according to all accounts, a complete breach between the brothers. When William made his Scottish will[27] in 1782 he left Long Calderwood not to John, who would have been the natural heir, but to his nephew, Matthew Baillie. This has been interpreted as spite on William's part, but there is another possible explanation. After her husband, James Baillie, died in 1778, Dorothy and her children went to live at Long Calderwood. William thought he was legally free to leave Long Calderwood to whom he liked, though, subsequently, it was found that this was not so.[28] He may have felt that by leaving it to Matthew Baillie, Dorothy was assured of a permanent home. John, established in London, was unlikely, had he owned it, ever to make use of Long Calderwood. The estate brought in little more than £70 per annum, which barely paid for its upkeep, so that John was deprived, in financial terms, of very little. After William's death, feeling an injustice had been done to John, Matthew Baillie made Long Calderwood over to him.

*   *   *   *   *   *   *

William was, however, of a quarrelsome and critical disposition, anxious for his own reputation, apparently jealous of the achievements of others, harshly critical of his colleagues, and controversy was a recurrent theme through his life.

He went to London as an assistant to William Smellie, specifically to gain experience in midwifery, but he stayed with Smellie less than a year. Though there is no evidence of any disagreement between them at this time, Hunter's readiness to move to work with James Douglas suggests that he may not have been altogether happy with Smellie. On the other hand, Hunter may have seen considerable social advantages in attaching himself to Douglas, who had an extensive practice amongst the aristocracy, and a considerable reputation as a scientist and scholar, positions that Smellie never aspired to. Later, the relationship between Hunter and Smellie was far from friendly. Tobias Smollett, a friend of both, wrote to Hunter

> I called at your house in hopes of getting a Dinner but my principal Design was to desire you will appoint a meeting with D$^{rs.}$ Smellie & Pitcairn, and I shall take care to attend you. Peter Gordon will wait on you tomorrow to receive your directions on that subject.
> Rainbow Coffee House.   Yours etc.
> Monday Oct 15, 1750.   T. Smollett.[29]

Some years later, Smellie again found grounds for complaints against Hunter, and

> Dr. Hunter Knowing it was without reason wrote to him to beg and insist upon a meeting at the British Coffee-house with their common friends D$^{rs.}$ Clephane and Pitcairn

but Smellie retired to Scotland without giving Hunter any satisfaction.

> This way I thought it safer than to have met D^r H^{rs} glib tongue and D^r P^{rns} good naturd and unsurly countinance; and also to prevent blood and battery which perhaps would have obliged me to have kept wandering 100 years before the boat man would receive me.[30]

The specific grounds for complaint are nowhere mentioned.

Hunter's time with the Douglases passed smoothly, and Mrs. Douglas provided a home not only for William but also for James when he was in London, and for John when he first came south. William was to continue his connections with the family after he had established his own home, for he was a witness to Mrs. Douglas's will. But even here, his treatment of the ne'r-do-well son, William George, though probably justified, provoked adverse criticism.

When Hunter came to employ assistants, serious problems arose, and not only with his brother John. One of the best documented quarrels is that with William Hewson, who replaced John as William's assistant and partner, for both have left statements of their side of the quarrel. Again, it has been suggested that it was Hewson's marriage to Mary Stevenson, daughter of Benjamin Franklin's landlady in London, that was the root of the quarrel. Indeed, this may have precipitated the final break, for Hunter undoubtedly thought that after marriage Hewson would devote less time to working for him. But the association between the two, which had run smoothly for some years, had begun to deteriorate before this. Hunter may have become jealous of Hewson's growing reputation as an anatomist, and the reward to him in 1769 of the Copley Medal by the Royal Society. John Hunter, who had no love for Hewson, accused him of taking credit for work which was essentially William Hunter's.[31] Yet it was William Hunter who in 1767 and 1768 gave to the Royal Society an account of the work that won Hewson the medal.

Hewson found Hunter's behaviour inexplicable, varying from condemnation to praise of the same work. He also found Hunter's strict and narrow interpretation of the terms of the contract of partnership between them unreasonable, for Hunter assumed ownership of all the anatomical preparations made by Hewson and all his experimental results, and claimed that all Hewson's time should be at his disposal. Furthermore, Hewson, who paid Hunter for his board and lodging, had also to pay him for the use of the museum and was not allowed access to Hunter's library.[32] But the reasons for breaking the partnership that Hunter gave to Benjamin Franklin, who attempted to mediate between them, were Hewson's absence for days on end without leave, of using for his own purposes bodies purchased by Hunter, of taking money from students against Hunter's orders, of not giving the lectures which, by the terms of contract, he was required to do, and that the lectures he did give were of so poor a quality that the students complained.[33]

Hewson departed and was replaced by William Cruickshank, an M.A. of Glasgow University, a competent linguist and a medical pupil of Dr. John Moore, a friend and former pupil of Hunter. Originally employed as a librarian, Cruickshank soon became his anatomical assistant and partner in the lectures. The use of the Great Windmill Street premises and of the museum collections was left to Cruickshank – with Matthew Baillie – in Hunter's will so that the anatomy lectures might be continued. But according to Joseph Adams, the relationship between the two was by no means without its problems, for

> It often required the mediation of mutual friends to preserve an intercourse extremely useful to one, and almost necessary to the other.[34]

Perhaps the work that Cruickshank did with John Hunter in 1776 on the regeneration of nerves,[35] and his obvious admiration for John, caused irritation to William. Or it might have been Cruickshank's publication in 1779, possibly without William's blessing and probably without his having seen the manuscript, of an appendix to Peter Clare's *Essay on the cure of abcesses,* for the Hunterian Library copy contains derogatory comments in Hunter's hand.

A number of artists were employed by Hunter, both for drawing and engraving his anatomical plates. By far the most important was Jan Van Rymsdyk, who was responsible for most of the original drawings for the *Anatomy of the human gravid uterus.* In the preface to this work Hunter acknowledged the help that he had received from Robert Strange, who had supervised the engraving of the plates and had himself engraved two of them. He did not, however, mention any of the artists by name, though the superb quality of Rymsdyk's drawings deserved special acknowledgement. Rymsdyk probably experienced additional sources of dissatisfaction, for he took his revenge on Hunter by characterising him as Dr. Ibis in *Museum Britanicum,* a book he wrote with his son, Andrew, in 1778. The ibis was the hieroglyphic of Mercury, god of messengers, thieves and of medicine. Rymsdyk considered he had

> been very useful as a designer and sacrificed my talents to a good purpose.... though I look on myself as a man that has been ill used and betrayed.

And addressing Dr. Ibis he added

> Pray now, as you was very lucky and did well in the world, what
> prejudice did I ever do you, why should you discourage me as a
> painter; was not I to live too? O, if I had a mind to expose you what
> we commonly call a whole length. But [the original printer supplied
> here six asterisks and two etcs. before a period].

But Rymsdyk was of a complaining nature: Italian and English artists, the Royal
Academy, most professional men, as well as William Hunter, drew from him
strictures and sour descriptions.

Hunter's medical quarrels, aired mainly in the *Medical Commentaries,* have been
adequately covered by Simmons. While the way in which he attacked the Monros
and Potts now appears disagreeable, it was not beyond the accepted way of
conducting controversies at that time, and from a study of student notes of
Hunter's early lectures it becomes more and more evident that, in relation to
Alexander Monro, *secondus,* and Percival Pott, right was on Hunter's side.

The ambiguous remark, added by John to the account of William's paper on
aneurisms in the first volume of *Medical Observations and Inquiries,* refers to a review
of this first volume in the *Monthly Review.*[36] The reviewer, John Douglas, no relation
of James Douglas, Hunter's teacher, attacked, amongst other things, William's
opinion that Paulus Aegineta had been the first to describe a true aneurism, and
gave that honour to Galen, accusing William of ignorance of the classical medical
authors. Douglas, in 1752, had set up in London as a teacher of anatomy when,
according to a partial friend

> those who knew his abilities were interested to oppose him, as
> conscious if ever he emerged into public notice he would snatch the
> palm from all of them. Accordingly they set about him with a more
> than sacradotal hatred.... and by every mean artifice endeavoured to
> depress him.[37]

Douglas's attack suggests that William took part, if he was not the leader of the
supposed opposition. The dispute was played out with unbelievable ferocity
between the *Monthly Review* and the *Critical Review* in which Tobias Smollett, as
editor, hurled invective at John Douglas on William Hunter's behalf, and the
subject was only laid to rest when John Douglas died in 1758.[38] But Hunter had
not finished with Paulus and aneurisms. He hunted out old Greek, Latin and
Arabic manuscripts in an attempt to prove that an error in transcription of the
manuscript from which Paulus's opinions were taken led to the confusion over
Paulus's description of aneurisms, a suggestion almost certainly correct. A study
pursued over ten years, involving correspondence with many scholars and
reading of ancient texts, it throws a side light on Hunter's scholarly interests.[39]

Always suspicious of being cheated, Hunter's dealings with collectors and his
agents in building up his museum were often acrimonious, and they must
have regretted becoming involved with him. Over the purchase of the Peralta
Collection of coins, which he believed he had been tricked into buying, he took
legal advice and found that the banker who had advanced the money for the
purchase could prosecute Louis Dutens, Hunter's agent in the purchase, to

recover it but could not touch Hunter himself, who refused to hand over the purchase price. In the end, the matter was amicably settled.[40] Poor Sir William Hamilton was not so fortunate. In 1782 he advised Hunter to buy a collection of coins for £333, which, when received, was found not to be worth £100, and was finally auctioned for £83.3.0. Hamilton paid back to Hunter the difference between what Hunter had paid for it and what it had made at the auction, leaving Sir William wishing 'to think as little as possible' about his loss of money.[41]

Mr Dawes offered to Hunter, for £220, the coins of his late father's collection that filled gaps in Hunter's cabinet, the duplicates to be returned, but Hunter, so Dawes held, took all the duplicates to the number, in some cases, of nine or ten of the valuable coins, and returned only those of little worth. Yet, as in all Hunter's correspondence in such matters, he justified his behaviour with brutal plainness and with a magnificent capacity of placing himself in the right.

> I explained what I meant viz No medal was a Duplicate where there was a *difference in the Dye;* and two were not duplicates, *when by injuries of preservation they were both necessary to make out the medal either in the figures or inscription.* You agreed. ..... Now Sir, I have kept my agreement with *an upright intention.* So far as I know I have not kept *one duplicate....* if our bargain should be void that will be a considerable regret, I mean the loss of time.[42]

Even when negotiations passed off agreeably, as in the purchase of John Swinerton's coin collection from his widow, who, in gratitude, sent Hunter, as well as the coins, some Greek vases from her husband's collection, in thanking her for them Hunter did not hesitate to tell her he did not think much of them.

> I am sorry the vases did not answer expectation but Knew not that any of them were crack'd when they were packed up.[43]

Hunter is said even to have quarrelled with his friend Tobias Smollett. Writing to William Cullen in 1758 about Cullen's London friends, he added:

> Smollett I know not what to say of. He has great virtues and has a turn for the warmest friendship. He is easily hurt and is very ready to take prejudices. There has been a great shyness between him and me, which his very kind behaviour to me when I was attacked by Douglas, Pott and Monro has yet scarcely conquered.[44]

But Smollett had borrowed money from Hunter, and this could well have been the cause of the shyness.[45]

At least with William Cullen there was never any hint of quarrel or disagreement, for he was 'the man to whom I owe and love most of all men in the world'.[46] Their correspondence, which continued to the end of William's life, remained always as between pupil and master. Cullen's affection for William probably was not shared by the rest of his family. Robina, Cullen's daughter, commented to John Thomson, who was collecting material for his life of William Cullen, that William Hunter never in ye course of his life sent my father ye most trifling present as a little acknowledgement of his Kindness either to himself or to his sister; and died at last, leaving a great property without leaving a farthing of legacy to my father, though he knew he was very far from rich.[47]

Yet, this was hardly fair to Hunter, who had offered to pay for the education of at least one of Cullen's sons.[48] Those who studied medicine became his pupils in London and were well aware of their obligation to him. One, possibly Archie, was employed for two years as his assistant.[49] Cullen himself considered the treatment of his sons 'the kindest possible'.[50]

☆   ☆   ☆   ☆   ☆   ☆

There was another side to William Hunter: he could be agreeable and amusing. When first he was in London, he associated mainly with other Scotsmen. Alexander Carlyle, the Minister of Inveresk, when in London, attended the weekly meetings of a club at the British Coffee-house, 'the members of which were mainly Scottish physicians from the city and court end of town....'.

> Hunter was gay and lively to the last degree, and often came in to us at nine o'clock fatigued and jaded. He had had no dinner, but supped on a couple of eggs and drank his glass of claret; for though we were a punch club, we allowed him a bottle of what he liked best. He repaid us with the brilliancy of his conversation. His toast was "May no English nobleman venture out of this world without a Scottish physician, as I am sure there are none who venture in".[51]

Not everyone found Hunter's conversation invariably brilliant: James Boswell, from time to time, met William Hunter at Sir John Pringle's levees. On one occasion

> Dr. Hunter fell to telling a long story of the bad behaviour of Dr. Harwood... I was patient for I suppose eight or ten minutes but the story was so uninteresting and Hunter spoke so tediously and so insipidly, that my mind was in such uneasiness as lungs are when in want of air.... I could endure it no longer and made my escape. Sir John Pringle who was happy to have a respite followed me into the passage.[52]

Soon Hunter's acquaintance extended beyond the circle of Scottish doctors. Probably through inheriting some of James Douglas's aristocratic patients, he was soon established in practice amongst the wealthy and influential. By 1759, when the game of 'loo had mounted to its zenith' and loo parties seemed to be part of convalescence for aristocratic ladies after childbirth, Horace Walpole wrote to George Montague

> We played at Lady Hertford's last week.... the last night of her lying in.... It is now adjourned to Mrs Fitzroy's whose child the town calls Pam-ela...[53] I proposed that instead of receiving cards for assemblies, one should send in a morning to Dr. Hunter's, the man-midwife, to know where there is loo that evening.[54]

Soon Hunter was as welcome in their drawing-rooms as at their bed-sides, as may be learnt from contemporary diaries, memoires and correspondence, though often editors have identified 'Dr. Hunter' as brother John.

It may have been through James Douglas that Hunter was introduced to the Hertfords, for Douglas had attended Lord Hertford's mother, Lady Conway. It was almost certainly Lady Hertford who introduced him to Horace Walpole. In 1760 she wrote to Walpole

> Lady Northumberland told me last night she had received a very agreeable present from you and admired it greatly. I want to beg one copy but as I own it is not for myself you may refuse me if you have the least inclination. The person I wish to give it to is Dr. Hunter, who is already a humble admirer of yours and must become still more so when he has had the pleasure of reading the *Fugitive Pieces*....[55]

Possibly Walpole declined to provide a copy for Hunter, for it does not occur in a contemporary catalogue of Hunter's Library. But friendship between the two men developed apace. Later he gave Hunter not one of his own works, but copies of both the French and English editions of Charles-Jean Francois Hénault's *Cornélie Vestale*, 1768, printed at Strawberry Hill. These were very rare books, because so few were printed. This was in return for Hunter's care of the wife of Walpole's steward.[56] Only the French edition survives in the Hunterian Library. Coins and politics were interests they had in common, and Walpole allowed Hunter to select from his rich Cabinet any coins that would be useful for filling up gaps in Hunter's Greek series.[57]

Friendship with Horace Walpole and Lord Hertford, and with Sir John Pringle, one of the Scottish doctors in London, none of whom appreciated Samuel Johnson, did not inhibit William Hunter from having a place in

> what was intellectually far the best society of the Kingdom, a society in which no talent or accomplishment was wanting and in which the art of conversation was cultivated with splendid success. There probably were not four talkers more admirable in four different ways than Johnson, Burke, Beauclerk and Garrick.[58]

Hunter, from surviving correspondence,[59] was well acquainted with three of these, and possibly also with Burke, who attended a course of his anatomy lectures.[60] And he makes appearances in Fanny Burney's Diary, was on terms of friendship with her father, Dr. Charles Burney, and was known but possibly not liked by Mrs Thrale.

Hunter had, at one time, a considerable interest in politics. 'By his attendance on Lady Esther Pitt [he] had frequent opportunities of seeing the great orator when he was ill with Gout'[61] and doubtless discussed with him more than his health. At first Hunter had sided with the Opposition, but as Hunter's relationship with the Royal Family passed from purely professional to that of friendship, it would have been embarrassing for him to be known as opposed to the King's opinions, nor did he miss opportunities of announcing his change of heart. After this Walpole's references to Hunter become rather sour. Writing to the Reverend William Mason, he related how

> Dr. Hunter, that Scotch night man[62] had the impudence t'other day to pour out at his anatomic lecture a more outrageous Smeltiad than Smelt himself, and imputed all our disgraces and ruin to the opposition. Burke was present, and said he had heard of political arithmetic but never before of political anatomy, yet for a Scot t'o dare thus in the heart of London, and be borne is proof enough that the nation itself is lost without redemption.[63]

Yet, for all Walpole's rantings against Hunter, they still continued to see each other. In 1780 he told Lady Ossory

> Two mornings ago they might have seen me receive first Dr. Hunter and a moment after, Lady Craven – a man midwife and so pretty a woman are very creditable; and yet alas he came to talk to me about Greek medals.[64]

Though Hunter, in 1778, wrote to a friend

> I told you I have taken my leave of politics and am sorry to say that as far as I am a judge this country deserves humiliation or rather a scurge.[65]

he moved in circles where political matters were freely discussed, and he could not help picking up the latest gossip. Just a week after the death of Lord Rockingham, in 1782, Dr. Johnson was able, through Hunter, to pass on the latest rumours.

> Dr. Hunter, who I take to have a very good intelligence, has just left me, and from him I learn only that all is yet uncertainty and confusion. Fox you know, has resigned, Burke's dismission is expected. I was particularly told that the Cavendishes were expected to be left out in the new settlement. The Dr. spoke, however, with very little confidence, nor do I believe that those who are now busy in the contest can judge of the event.[66]

Hunter is often represented as a misogynist, and from this is believed to have stemmed his dislike of marriage. Mrs. Thrale, who was hurt by Hunter's neglect of her recommendation of a friend as wet nurse for the queen,[67] quoted several times, with relish, Sir Richard Jebb's verses on Hunter's embalming of Martin van Butchell's wife.[68]

> To do his wife's dead Corps peculiar Honour
> Van Butchell wish'd to have it turned to stone,
> Hunter just cast his Gorgon looks upon her,
> And in a twinkling see the thing is done.

William Hewson, writing to a friend about his marriage, said

> My friend Dr. Hunter was much afraid it would spoil me as an anatomist.... to tell you a secret I do think the doctor's fears are not

groundless. I find the living much more agreeable than the dead.
My friend the Dr. indeed when he speaks of women, for himself,
says to a man of 50 there is no difference.[69]

This was just a pose on Hunter's part, for his relationship with various women,
particularly the Countess of Hertford, does not bear this out. He was constantly
at her house and ready to do her commands. He bought government stock for
her when she was in Paris, and took out power of attorney to act on her behalf
when she was in Ireland.[70] Nor did she hesitate to ask him to undertake other
errands for her.

> I gave orders for some paper Madam de Mirepoix wanted for a
> room, while I was in London and desired Dr. Hunter to take care to
> send it to her as soon as it was made.[71]

He even possessed a portrait of her by Alexandre Roslin. And that was not the
only female portrait he possessed. He probably bought from Sir William
Maynard, in 1771,[72] Joshua Reynold's portrait of Lady Maynard, a patient of his,
on whose behalf he persuaded the elder Pitt to release Nurse Carruthers,
employed to look after his second son, so that she could help Lady Maynard in
the troubles of her confinement. Hunter also had an interest in a portrait of Lady
St. Aubyn, who gave him the collection of Cornish minerals, for in Joshua
Reynold's ledger for 1761 is an entry: 'Lady St. Aubyn, paid for by Dr. Hunter
£10.10.0 though the entry was subsequently cancelled.[73]

Indeed, it is mainly in the diaries and letters of women that Hunter appears,
and though it is generally in connection with health and childbearing, he figures
also on more frivolous occasions. Lady Holland tells how

> I went in the evening to Lady Blandford.... I made her laugh with
> telling her that I had got a great many sore fingers with pruning my
> rose trees and that some of the thorns had got so deep into the flesh
> that I had consulted Dr. Hunter, as I thought he might be as skilful
> in delivering one of thorns as he was on some other occasions. She
> said it was the first time she heard of his being consulted about
> fingers.[74]

Hunter it was who attended Lady Holland in 1774 when she was dying of
cancer. He refused to allow William Rowley, who claimed to be able to cure
almost everything, including cancer, to see her, saying

> he thought it would be highly imprudent to admit a *stranger*; that he
> [Dr. Rowley] might increase her Ladyship's *pain*, and that Dr.
> Hunter did not think it possible that any relief could be obtained.[75]

In William Rowley, Hunter met one 'as implacable in resentment and
determined in contempt'[76] as himself. Rowley published two letters to William
Hunter *on the dangerous tendency of medical vanity,*[77] accusing Hunter of causing Lady
Holland's death. Hunter was certainly right in the diagnosis of Lady Holland's
condition and Rowley received no support in his accusations. Monk was later to
write of Rowley 'neither his character or career were of a kind we delight to dwell
on'.[78]

*   *   *   *   *   *

Undoubtedly, Hunter's greatest success with women was in his progress to friendship with the queen.

29 October 1766.

Sir
> Her Majesty would like to see you at her house at a little after three, but you must not mention that you was sent for, only that you want to see Prince Frederick as you heard he was in town.
> I am Sr.
> Y^r Obed Ser
> M. Ancaster.[79]

Though Horace Walpole described Hunter as 'Queen's favorite', this was not to suggest any impropriety in their relationship. The note probably indicated only a desire to consult Hunter privately on some matter of the health of the family, possibly that of the King, who at that time was thought to be suffering from consumption.

Though Hunter was never called in to attend the King, he was kept so well informed of the King's state of health, either by the Queen or by the King's doctors, that the Duchess of Argyll applied to him for the latest news on that subject.[80]

Not only was he in favour with the Queen, but the King also was most kindly disposed towards him. It has been suggested that the King's present to him of the second edition of James Beattie's *An essay on the nature and inimitability of truth, in opposition to sophistry and sceptism* (1771) was a warning to Hunter not to embrace the opinions of David Hume which were abhorrent to the King. But other presents were less pointed: he gave Hunter, to fill a gap in his coin collection, an Athenian gold piece of such rarity that Eckhel, the great authority on coins, could not believe it was genuine.[81] The Queen gave him an elephant and a zebra that died in her menagerie.[82] In return, Hunter begged them to accept the gift of a turtle.[83]

His friendship with the Royal Family laid Hunter open to approaches by various people to obtain favours or present petitions to the King on their behalf. Samuel Johnson asked him to present to the King on his behalf a copy of *A journey to the Western Isles of Scotland.*[84] Hunter refused to present, through the Queen, a petition to the King for mercy for the worthless son of a poor woman in Glasgow, as the case had already been properly presented to the King.[85] In another case, he again refused to take action.

College of Glasgow 20 Jan. 1778

Dr. Sir
It gave me real concern to hear lately that one of my colleagues had wrote to you desiring you to addres his M——— about our Societies raising a Regiment. That Gentleman is apt to be rather forward & presuming upon his own Judgement: for as far as I know he had not consulted with anyone of the Professors when he wrote that Letter. We are all loyal and zealous Subjects and will be willing to do

anything in our Power to promote the Public Interest But our taking
the Funds of the Society in the manner proposed is a matter that
required the most Serious Deliberation . . .
    It gave me real pleasure to understand from your friend Dr.
Baillie that you had wisely taken no steps in consequence of the
letter: I give you the trouble of this to assure you that I, and so far as
I know, all the Professors consider themselves as obliged to you for
your Caution and Prudence in this matter . . .

Your most obed^t & Humble Servt
Will: Leechman.[86]

William Hunter was probably acquainted with David Hume through John
Clephane, and later through Lord Hertford. Hume went to France with Lord
Hertford as his secretary, and Hunter corresponded with Hume in Paris.[87] When
it was suggested that Hume should join Lord Hertford in Ireland, James Trail,
who had been chaplain to the Embassy in Paris and had then been made Bishop
of Down and Connor, wrote to Hunter, asking him to dissuade Hume from
coming to Ireland

> where his character as a philosopher is an object of universal disgust,
> not to say detestation, in this country and his historical character,
> especially where Ireland and the Stewarts are concerned is excessively
> disliked.[88]

Whether or not Hunter spoke to Hume is not known, for Hume, for his own
reasons, declined to go to Ireland.
    His collecting brought him a wide circle of acquaintances, from Lord Bute and
Lord Sandwich to John Bedford of Bridgend, Glamorganshire, an ironfounder,
and John Jeans, the 'fossilist' whom Samuel Johnson met on his journey to the
Western Isles. He had friends and established connections with dealers and
collectors on the continent.
    In 1768 Hunter wrote to William Cullen: 'I am pretty much acquainted with
most of our best artists and live in friendship with them'.[89] This was the year
he was appointed Professor of Anatomy at the Royal Academy, but his friendship with artists predates this. Both Allan Ramsay and Robert Strange were
Scotsmen. It may have been as a student in Edinburgh that Hunter first met
Robert Strange, apprenticed to Richard Cooper, engaged in engraving anatomical
plates for Alexander Monro *primus,* and Allan Ramsay was also in Edinburgh at that
time. He knew them well enough by 1759 to be asked to mediate in a quarrel
between the two when Strange refused to engrave Ramsay's portraits of the
Prince of Wales and Lord Bute.[90] Ramsay later painted Hunter's portrait, and
Strange supervised the engravings for the *Anatomy of the human gravid uterus.*
Robert Mylne, architect of Blackfriars, was also originally from Edinburgh. He
designed Hunter's Great Windmill Street premises, and was connected to the
Hunter family by marrying the sister of John Hunter's wife. William Hunter also
promoted with Glasgow City Council the interest of Robert's brother, William,
by presenting to them William's design for a bridge over the Clyde – the Jamaica
Street Bridge, which the city contracted to built in 1768.[91]
    Hunter's connection with William Hogarth and the St. Martin's Lane

Academy, where he first gave anatomy lectures to artists, may have been established by Bernard Baron. He was an engraver brought from France to help Claude Dubosc with his engravings of the story of Ulysses from designs by Rubens possessed by Dr. Mead. Both Dubosc and Baron worked for James Douglas, and Baron also engraved for William Hogarth.

There is ample evidence that William supported, financially, his sister Dorothy and her husband, their son, Matthew Baillie, whose medical education he undertook, and even John Hunter. Hunter's financial aid to Tobias Smollett is well known. But in the surviving correspondence there is no record of private charity or kindness. There are no letters from humble people thanking him for help or support as there are amongst James Douglas's papers. But Baillie, in sorting William's letters, may have destroyed them. Hewson records that Hunter would not treat those who could not pay his full fee.[92] He subscribed to a few charities such as that 'for the encouragement of British troops in Germany and North America'. He was a governor of the British Lying-in Hospital, which entailed a donation of at least thirty guineas, and also of St. George's Hospital, which required a yearly subscription. This hardly adds up to a picture of a kind and generous man. Though, if John Hunter's remarks are accepted, William performed his charitable acts 'in the quietest way possible'.

Allan Ramsay describes himself as 'well acquainted with Hunter's benevolent disposition'.[93] Lord Suffolk lauded William's 'humanity & attention and sensibility of heart' in the events leading up to the death of Lady Suffolk.[94] But a slight cloud is cast over this by the suggestion, though on no firm evidence, that Hunter was responsible for her ladyship's death by leaving the placenta too long in the uterus.[95] There must have been qualities of friendship and generosity that attracted such men as John Fothergill, Henry Fielding and William Cullen, and women like the Queen and the Countess of Hertford to him. But only in one surviving letter is there presented a picture of William Hunter in kind and happy mood. Lord Newborough wrote on 15 December 1782 from Florence, where he had gone with his young son after the death of his wife earlier in the year

> Your old friend, Young Monkey, joins me in wishing most sincerely you may pass many happy Christmas Days with the Same Good Spirit as that you pass'd upon the Ice at Hampstead with him.[96]

Not all Hunter's patients were respectably married women. He looked after Miss Ray for Lord Sandwich,[97] and Robert Walpole, son of Horatio Walpole of Wolterton, sent his mistress to him because he believed that Hunter would receive her 'with care, candour and privacy'.[98] But was he right in that belief? For Hunter used to relate, with details that made identification a possibility, how

> During the American war, he was consulted by the daughter of a Peer, who confessed herself pregnant, and requested his assistance; he advised her to retire for a time to the house of some confidential friend; she said that was impossible, for her father would not suffer her to be absent from him a single day. Some of the servants were therefore let into the secret, and the Doctor made his arrangements with the Foundling Hospital for the reception of the child for which he was to pay £100. – The lady was desired to weigh well if she could

bear pain, without alarming the family with her cries; she said 'Yes', – and kept her word. At the usual period she was delivered, not of one child only but of twins. The Doctor bearing the two children, was conducted by a French servant through the Kitchen, and left to ascend the area steps to the street. Luckily the lady's-maid recollected that the door of the area might perhaps be locked, and she followed the doctor just in time to prevent his being detained at the gate. He deposited the children at the Foundling Hospital and paid for each £100. The father of the children was a Colonel in the army, who went with his regiment to America, and died there. The mother afterwards married a person of her own rank.[99]

Gossiping and spreading rumours must have been a failing of William Hunter. Horace Walpole, having heard some chatter about Lord Harcourt, wrote to him

> I wish you as rich as Croesús my dear Lord but Impatient as I am to see you call out all the beauties of Nuneham, I had rather see you dig your own garden than not have you a *Harcourt sans reproche;* I mean that even Dr. Hunter should not be able to invent a blemish that would stick.[100]

With this review of Hunter's failings it is hard to accept that he was 'of principles to be depended upon at all times for doing right'. And this is driven home by another story against Hunter, told by Horace Walpole. It concerned the Duchess of Gloucester who

> at her first husband Lord Waldegrave's death, had a disorder in her breast, which was attended by other circumstances which made her believe and declare herself with child. At the end of six months, finding herself not pregnant, she ordered her man-midwife, Dr. Hunter, who had told her she was *not,* to acquaint Lord and Lady Elizabeth Waldegrave, that they might be out of their suspense, and assure themselves that they would enjoy the title and estate. Dr. Hunter advised her not to send such a message, as he *might be* mistaken. She followed his advice – but he himself went and acquainted Lady Elizabeth Waldegrave with the very secret that he might have the merit of betraying it, instead of letting his patient act in the generous and friendly manner she intended.[101]

*   *   *   *   *   *

Whatever the shortcomings of his character, Hunter's scientific achievements were undoubtedly very considerable. Simmons catalogues his publications and briefly describes their contents, but gives little indication of their quality.

The roots of much of William Hunter's work lie in the interests of James Douglas, Hunter's teacher. Douglas published only a small fraction of the work he had been engaged in. But William Hunter had access to, and eventually acquired, all Douglas's papers and drawings.

In 1725 George I gave Douglas £500 to help him publish an Osteology and a treatise on the diseases of women.[102] At the time of Douglas's death, the Osteology was almost ready for publication. Hunter had worked on the Osteology, either under Douglas or later when he had thoughts of publishing it posthumously,[103] for the labelling of the plates was extensively carried out by him. If published, it would have been a magnificent work, for not only would it have comprised life-sized drawings of all the bones, separate and articulated, but also an extensive text covering the structure and development of bones and their diseases, together with a history of osteology and osteological figures. Part of the work covered a very detailed consideration of the knee joint, and Douglas had been the first to describe the succuli mucosi whose secretions lubricate the surfaces of joints.[104] This work could well have been the basis of Hunter's first paper to the Royal Society in 1743 on articular cartilages and their diseases, for it fits well into the pattern of James Douglas's work.

There are records of Douglas's interest in ducts round the eye,[105] and in the thoracic duct.[106] He left a vast collection of writings on the history of aneurisms[107] which first makes the point that Paulus undoubtedly described a true aneurism. William Cheselden records that Hunter made many dissections of hernias for James Douglas, for a projected work on the subject.[108] Almost certainly, Hunter's interest in the gravid uterus must have been stimulated by Douglas's large collection of dissection notes and drawings of the gravid uterus in all stages of pregnancy. Hunter has been credited with being the first to describe the round ligament and *linea alba* in the female, but both these were clearly described by James Douglas.[109]

After Hunter's death, three papers by him were found and read to the Society of Collegiate Physicians and published in *Medical Observations and Inquiries,* volume 6. Two of these are amongst his most important publications.

Three cases of malformation of the heart reveals the extent of his biological thinking, an early realisation of natural selection operating on random variations to bring about changes in a species.

Many animals from the imperfections of their fabric, are necessary to perish before the common natural period. This is compensated by a great superfluity in the number, and so it is also in the vegetable kingdom. As in vegetables too, the parent generally produces a species like itself, but sometimes a different constitution, whether better or worse. What ever may happen in a particular instance or with regard to an individual, the most perfect and sound animal upon the whole, will have the best chance of living to procreate others of his kind: in other words the best breed will prevail: and the monstrous constitution, and that which is defective, or of such a fabrick as necessarily to breed disease, will be cut off. The most perfect constitution will be preserved.... the sound constitution will have the preference in procreation and the defective, weak, or diseased line will be wearing out.

On the Uncertainty of Signs of Murder in the case of bastard children was destined to become an early classic in forensic medicine. In it Hunter stressed the impossibility of determining whether a bastard child, who had taken air into its lungs, had subsequently been murdered or died from natural causes. He argued strongly for the consideration of the mental state of these women, and shows a humanity which some of Hunter's other activities might suggest was not one of his characteristics. Hunter had, from time to time, been called to give evidence in such cases.

He was also called as expert witness in other trials. Samuel Clossy, a one-time pupil of Hunter, relates that

> Lord Burlington's Cook was assaulted by two Persons in the night at a place called Bayswater, who fractured his skull into Shivers; on the morning following he was brought into St. Georges [Hospital] having so much understanding left, to tell the case and that he had wounded one of them in the Breast as he lay on his back; the man died that evening; and an account of the affair being sent to Mr. Fielding; in some days after a Soldier of the Guards was apprehended having just such a wound as the cook described and sent to Mr. Fielding who summoned Dr. Hunter to inspect the wound and the parts divided, Dr. Hunter easily concluded that it was given from beneath, this opinion then, with concomitant Proofs, frightened him into a confession and both himself and companion received the reward of their deeds.[110]

In 1760 William Hunter saved from execution for murder a servant of the elder Pitt, by proving that the fatal wound that he gave William Robinson, a chairman, must, from its position and nature, have been inflicted in self defence against Robinson's attack on him.[111]

The Douglas Cause was a matter of interest to Hunter. He expressed privately to Andrew Stuart, one of the lawyers retained by the Hamiltons, his medical reasons for believing Lady Jane Stewart was a fraud. Counsel wished to quote the opinion 'of so great an authority' but were doubtful if they had Hunter's permission to do so.[112] But his opinions may well have influenced their arguments.

Hunter's excursions into natural history were anatomical, in his descriptions of the Nyl-Ghau and moose-deer, or Orignal. But his most important contribution to biology lay in his promotion of the researches of John Hunter, William Hewson and William Cruickshank into the comparative anatomy of the lymphatic system of fish, reptiles and birds. Indeed, whether it was the lymphatic system, the development of the testes, the structure of the gravid uterus or other organs, William had then examined in the human and compared against the structures in a whole range of mammals, birds and reptiles. William gave John his introduction to comparative anatomy, a study which John was himself to pursue with incredible industry in both vertebrates and invertebrates according to class, size, age, sex and environment. His conclusions were illustrated by the series of specimens in his museum, material with which Charles Darwin must have been acquainted through his friendship with Richard Owen when he was Curator of the Hunterian Museum at the Royal College of Surgeons of England.

Hunter was inclined to accept, on the authority of von Haller, that the mammalian ovary produced only a secretion, not an organized ovum. He was, however, willing to finance the experiments of William Cruickshank which confirmed beyond any doubt the earlier work of De Graaf, for Cruickshank correlated, in rabbits, the rupture of the Graafian follicles with the release of ova from the ovary, and then traced their passage down the Fallopian tubes into the uterus, where, after eight days, he could detect development in the ovum, and by the ninth its attachment to the uterus wall. These experiments carried out in 1778, were not published till 1797 in the *Philosophical Transactions.*[113] It is doubtful if he actually identified the ovum within the Graafian follicle. Karl Ernst von Baer was the first definitely to make this observation.[114] Von Baer was fortunate to have used the ovary of a bitch in which the follicle is relatively large and clear, the egg within standing out because of its dense cytoplasm. In spite of this, von Baer believed the whole follicle to form the mammalian ovum. Cruickshank correctly described the follicle as the calyx within which the ovum was formed. Hunter's contribution to mammalian embryology, both through his own work and by sponsoring that of William Cruickshank, has not been fully appreciated.

Except for the few cases published in his papers and some others mentioned in his lectures, little record survives of Hunter's wide practice both in surgery and medicine. William was a surgeon for nearly fifteen years. John supplements Simmon's brief mention of the fact by recording some of Hunter's surgical activities. Whether he liked it or not, since he had to earn his living that way, he applied his mind to it, invented new surgical instruments,[115] and, from his anatomical knowledge, devised the best ways of carrying out various surgical manipulations. And surgery was included in his anatomical lectures. As to his success as an obstetrician, there can be no doubt, otherwise he would not have been so widely employed. Part of his success was, undoubtedly, in letting Nature take her way. He did make mistakes which he, or others, recorded but he learnt from his mistakes, for he made them the basis of warnings to his pupils.

His ideas on Materia Medica we learn from William Cruickshank:

> Dr. Hunter's belief in Physic was reduced to a small compass. He said he was sure of three things, that sulphur would cure the itch, mercury the pox and the Bark an intermittent fever.[116]

His medical and scientific reputation has suffered partly because no collected edition of his works was ever published, and few people have bothered to hunt out and read the separate papers in the *Philosophical Transactions* and *Medical Observations,* and the appendices that he added to publications by his colleagues. Matthew Baillie, in 1794, completed and published a manuscript he found amongst his uncle's papers, *A description of the human gravid uterus,*[117] which supplements the *Anatomy of the human gravid uterus* and William Cruickshank gathered together the work done under William Hunter's direction by John Hunter, William Hewson and himself on the lymphatic system.[118] But both Cruickshank, who died in 1800, and Matthew Baillie were too engaged in their own researches to undertake any more extensive act of homage to the man who had trained them up and set them on the path to fame.

❊   ❊   ❊   ❊   ❊   ❊

Hunter's reputation as a lecturer was so great that not only medical students but such men as Adam Smith,[119] Edward Gibbon,[120] Edmund Burke, William Robertson[121] and, doubtless, many others, attended them. Alexander Carlyle records that he and Robinson expressed a wish to be admitted to a lecture.

> He appointed us a day, and gave us one of the most elegant, clear, and brilliant lectures on the eye that any of us ever heard.[122]

Unfortunately, Hunter never published any of his lectures. After his death was found the manuscript of

> Two Introductory Lectures
> by Dr. Hunter
> Read at his New Theatre on the
> first and second day of Oct[r], 1767[123]

with additions and corrections that had been added through the years.[124] These were published by his trustees in 1784, described as the introduction to his last course of anatomical lectures.[125] They could still be read today with profit by medical students. The two lectures relate to the history and uses of anatomy and how it should be studied.

The only knowledge of how he actually taught the subject is obtained from students' notes of his lectures. These date from 1749 to 1781. Teaching anatomy over more than thirty years, at a time when the subject was developing and changing, it is not surprising that the lectures changed with the years. Hunter incorporated into his lectures the only account ever given of much of his own research work, on such varied subjects as the physical and chemical properties of insect, frog and human blood; the volume of air taken into and expelled from the lungs at each breath; whether, when a man is hanged, he dies from asphyxia or from blood being cut off from the brain; why it is more difficult to revive animals than humans after drowning.[126] Some of his recorded observations were remarkably perceptive. In relation to cancer he concluded that

> the greater number of those unhappy women who have been afflicted with either of these disorders in the breast or uterus have never born any child or have neglected to give it suck.[127]

He also recorded the observations of his assistants.

> Mr C[ruickshank] believes an ovum comes to the uterus every month and is washed away by a flood of blood.[128]

though history credits Gendrin as the first to make this suggestion in 1839.[129]

It is possible, from his lectures, to follow the development of his ideas on the anatomy of the gravid uterus, and many other subjects. All this, in spite of the fact that students often recorded only what interested them, which was often not what was most significant, and they frequently misunderstood what they were being taught. But so many sets of student notes have survived that it is possible to arrive at a reasonably accurate idea of the contents of his lectures.

He obviously had a flair for holding the students' attention with amusing stories, like that of the 'lady of fortune whose husband was unhappy on account of her not breeding'. She faked a pregnancy and miscarriage, which Hunter diagnosed as a piece of boiled liver. But he did not give her away to her husband 'who was very sorry for her and sent her to Bath to recuperate'.[130] He expounded the complicated anatomy of the ear by taking, as it were, a walk through it,[131] possibly with the aid of wall diagrams, and his anatomical preparations were an essential part of his teaching. He must often have stressed his point by exaggeration, for after a horrific story of a mortification of the vagina he added

> Now, you will say Gentlemen, this is one of *Hunter's cases*, but if you do say so, it will not be so much use as I mean it, because there has not been the least circumstance exaggerated.[132]

Hunter certainly worked his pupils hard, for they were lectured to for two hours a day, six days a week. The course which originally had been given twice each year, one course before the other after Christmas, was finally one course from September to May. It is not surprising that occasionally a pupil slipped away to attend the theatre.[133]

> He lived at the period when Garrick was in his zenith, he soon discovered that he stood no chance with the actor, for when ever Garrick *lectured,* the *anatomical lectures* were neglected. In vain did the Doctor preach to the pupils the immorality of attending theatres and the impropriety of neglecting him, it was of no avail. Romeo's Apothecary, and Dr. Last were the only medical characters to spend the evening with, and for the rest they thought Macbeth sufficient authority to "throw physic to the dogs". For this reason, and this reason alone, the anatomical lectures were afterwards given in the middle of the day.[134]

Lecturing in the afternoon from 2–4 o'clock would have left him free to respond to Sir John Fielding's appeal on 4 December, 1778:

> Sir John Fielding presents his compliments to Dr. Hunter and acquaints him that "The Comedy of the Good Natured Man" written by the late Mr. Henry Fielding will be performed at Drury Lane next Monday, being the Author's Widow's night.
> He was your old and sincere friend. There is no other of his works left unpublished. This is the last opportunity you will have of shewing any respect to his memory as a Genius so that I hope you will send all your pupils, all your patients, all your Friends, & everybody else to the play that night, by which means you will indulge your benevolent feelings & your sentiments of Friendship.[135]

For, at least in his early days in London, William Hunter was as fond of the theatre as his pupils.

His relationship with his students seems to have resulted in no recorded disputes or quarrels, except with the American, John Morgan, who demonstrated to the Royal Medical Society in Paris the making of corroded anatomical specimens without admitting that he had learnt the method from William Hunter, who had himself learnt it from Frank Nicholl.[136] One of his pupils, the American, William Shippen, if he did not regard Hunter with affection, at least admired him sufficiently to call his first-born son after him.[137] But there is no indication that he ever established with his pupils the friendly and affectionate relationships that developed between William Cullen and many of his pupils, or even between John Hunter and the young men who worked with him. But William took an interest in, and occasionally entertained, his pupils, particularly if they were sons of old Glasgow friends. William Hamilton, son of Thomas Hamilton, Professor of Anatomy and Botany at Glasgow in 1777, wrote to his father:

> I would have wrote you on Saturday night but went to Dr. Hunter's lecture and after the class the Dr. asked me and G. Reid who was along with me to come and eat an oyster with him and we sat till eleven.... he was vastly chatty with us at supper. G. Reid and he seem to be very intimate he has breakfasted once or twice and dined with him.[138]

G. Reid was George Reid, son of Professor Thomas Reid of Glasgow University. Hunter was later to use his influence to get George Reid appointed a hospital mate in the army in America.[139]

Drafts of Hunter's lectures on anatomy to the Royal Academy[140] have survived. Only those aspects of anatomy that were of interest to the artist were dealt with. He went on to consider the artist's rôle in relation to Nature, holding that Nature was always superior to Art. This was an opinion that Sir Joshua Reynolds disputed in his third Discourse to the Academy in 1770; 'there are excellencies in the art of painting beyond what is commonly called the imitation of Nature'. In later lectures Hunter was to accept that 'ideal form' was a valid concept for the artist. Hunter told the Academy that painting and sculpture were 'arts which have always been one of my highest pleasures', and his own collection of pictures shows an individual artistic taste. Numbering amongst his friends artists like Sir Joshua Reynolds, James Barry and William Hogarth, and a critic like Horace Walpole, he must have discussed art theory with them and may have read a little on the subject, for his library contained some relevant books, but not many. Hunter's real contribution to the Royal Academy was not his ideas of artistic perfection but the fostering of fresh enthusiasm for professional standards in artistic anatomy for Robert Knox, writing in the 1850s, summed up the British academic painters of the period as the 'Anatomical School'.[141]

* * * * * *

There is no clear indication of Hunter's motives for building up his museum. As his wealth accumulated, presumably he wished to convert it to tangible form rather than keep it in stocks and shares that might well not maintain their value. Land and country estates, in which it was common to invest wealth, were, by the eighteenth century, in short supply, and William's attempts at such an investment had come to nothing. Though some of his friends, like John Fothergill, had country estates, for a professional man whose work was centred in London, they could not have been a very satisfactory possession. Sir Hans Sloane, Richard Mead and Antony Askew, all medical men, built up famous museums or libraries, so Hunter was in no way out of the ordinary. He was extraordinary only in the extent and variety of his collections. Nor was his museum in any sense a collection of curiosities, but had direct relevance to current interests and was organised and catalogued in a rational manner. He took advice from experts over purchases and gave what time he could to the collections. He was generous in making his treasures available to friends, and even friends of friends, to help them with their various studies.

There is no need to explain the anatomical preparations, for they were essential for the teaching of anatomy. When bodies were hard to obtain, and some students could not afford the extra expense of becoming a dissecting pupil, the preparations helped to demonstrate clearly what might not be seen to advantage in the dissection prepared for the lecture. They were even more important in demonstrating pathological conditions. After Hunter's death, Glasgow University was impatient to get possession of them, and their arrival in Glasgow resulted in a considerable increase in the number of medical students at the university.[142]

Much of the material illustrated in Hunter's *Anatomy of the human gravid uterus* and in his other papers survives amongst the preparations.[143] Matthew Baillie, who came to be regarded as the father of morbid anatomy, was able to base much of his work on material in the museum,[144] and this has served to record some specimens that have since disappeared through loss or decay. Perhaps it was as well for Baillie that William Hunter was not alive to hear Baillie credited with having been the first to point out that what was believed to be a polypus or growth in the heart causing death was a mass of coagulated fibrin formed after death,[145] a conclusion that Hunter had for years taught in his lectures,[146] and a specimen illustrating this is still in existence (10.2 in the Anatomy Museum).

Since the seventeenth century attempts to construct a geological history of the earth had greatly stimulated an interest in minerals and fossils, both of which were collected by Hunter. George Fordyce used Hunter's collections for his work on the chemical composition of minerals. He worked out a rational system of mineral classification, a system he applied in arranging and cataloguing Hunter's minerals for him.[147]

Hunter himself, in his papers to the Royal Society on the *Incognitum* and on the fossils in a piece of rock from Gibraltar, demonstrated how important accurate anatomical knowledge was in the identification of fossil material, and added his weight to arguments in favour of the extinction of animal species, an idea by no means generally accepted. Hunter's *Incognitum* paper has been overlooked and it is Cuvier who is generally credited with applying careful anatomical investigations to prove, in 1798, that the bones of the *Incognitum,* or, as he called it, the *Mastodon,* from Ohio were not those of an elephant but of an extinct large animal.[148]

The insect collection, built up over many years and from many sources included material from the Cook Voyages[149] and later over 900 specimens bought from Thomas Yates' collection in 1782.[150] It was arranged for Hunter by J.C. Fabricius,[151] and used by him to establish a number of insect species.[152]

Hunter's shell collection contained the magnificent collection assembled by John Fothergill, and considered as second only to that of the Duchess of Portland. Under the terms of Fothergill's will, Hunter bought this for £1,000. When the Duchess's collection was auctioned in 1786 it made £11,546. 14. 0.[153] Fothergill's collection, like that of the Duchess of Portland, contained many shells brought back from Captain Cook's voyages, but Hunter himself may have acquired Cook shells, either by gift or purchase, for he also possessed an extensive collection of 'curiosities from the South Seas'.[154]

Coins had long established themselves as important source material for the reconstruction of ancient history. Though Hunter became a Fellow of both the English and Scottish Societies of Antiquaries, it was as a collector and not as an ancient historian that he could claim to be an antiquarian. His friend, Charles Combe, advised him on purchases and ordered his collections. A complete catalogue of them, in seven volumes, was planned. Only Charles Combe's *Nummorum veterum populorum et urbium,* 1782, an enormous advance in recording coins, was ever published. *The Gentleman's Magazine,* 1782, was happy to announce to its readers that it was

> proposed to publish the noble collection of Saxon coins preserved in Dr. Hunter's collection, illustrated with notes and historical observations. This work is intended to elucidate a part of English history at present involved in much uncertainty and obscurity.... The description of the coins, we understand, will be by the Rev. Mr. Southgate.

But neither this nor the other five catalogues ever appeared. Hunter's Coin Collection was regarded as the most extensive collection in private hands, and its potential for research into ancient history was immense. This was the reason that efforts were made, after Hunter's death, to buy the collection from Glasgow University and keep it in London.[155]

Hunter's collection of pictures was not extensive, between 50 and 60 all told, and was probably acquired primarily as furnishings for the walls of his house. It contained family portraits, and portraits of famous medical men, William Harvey, John Radcliffe, Walter Charlton and John Arbuthnot, and of Sir Isaac Newton, together with pictures of animals commissioned from George Stubbs. Hunter also acquired, mainly from sales of pictures collected by Robert Strange, a representative collection of seventeenth-century Italian works, much in favour at that time. But he did show independence of choice in the purchase of a number of Dutch and Flemish pictures. These included Rembrandt's sketch, *Entombment of Christ,* a picture, by any reckoning, of outstanding importance, bought for twelve guineas, and a fine Philip Konincke landscape, though bought by Hunter as a Rembrandt. But of all the pictures in the collection, his three Chardins provide the most striking example of his personal taste, for at that time Chardin was unknown and unblessed by English critics.[156]

Except for medical books, both contemporary and ancient, some of which came from James Douglas's library and which were of importance to Hunter professionally, it is difficult to see, in Hunter's book-collecting, anything more than his desire to 'possess a copy of every curious book on the face of the earth'.[157] Some 10,000 volumes, including 534 incunabula, amongst which were 10 Caxtons, 2,300 sixteenth-century publications and, in addition, 650 manuscripts, many of great interest and value, cover virtually all fields of learning and the library is surprisingly rich in early books on North America. Hunter was interested in the early printing of Greek characters, and in Cicero, Virgil, Terence and Chaucer, on all of which he left extensive notes,[158] and on which he corresponded with other scholars. A list of books borrowed from the library records[159] not only his willingness to lend but also the interests of his friends. Besides medical colleagues borrowing medical works, Benjamin Franklin borrowed several works on Mary, Queen of Scots; Dr. Warren, the 'Bramin' Code of Laws; Dr. Musgrave, the Euripides in Greek capitals; Benjamin West, various art books, while the St. Aubyn family made general use of the library.

William, on building up his museum and library, spent a vast fortune. Exactly how he amassed this fortune is uncertain, for his bank account from 1754, which survives at Drummond's Branch of the Royal Bank of Scotland, while revealing much about Hunter's financial activities, leaves much tantalisingly unexplained. In 1756 he was credited with only £230; the following year £1,000; in 1759 with £2,222.8.0; in 1761, £15,424.10.3 and in 1762, £28,148.13.3. Though this was a time when his practice was expanding rapidly, and he was well established as a successful teacher of anatomy, neither of these activities can account for his remarkable growth in wealth. Hewson who, through the terms of his contract, took first one third and then half the profit from the anatomy classes, in 1770 received only £270,[160] indicating that Hunter cleared only £540 for his teaching in that year, and earlier the profit may well have been less. His appointment to the queen brought him £200 per annum, and his professorship at the Royal Academy, £30. It is impossible to determine from his bank account what he made from his practice, most credits being recorded only as 'cash received'.

But what his account does reveal is his extensive dealings in government lotteries, and how much he played the market, buying and selling both government and East India Company stock. Unfortunately, no records survive of prize-winners in the government lotteries for the years 1759-1763 when Hunter was buying both lottery tickets and stock, which entitled him to further tickets. In 1761 he bought 50 tickets and some £10,000 of stock, and winnings on this may well have formed the foundation of his wealth. By 1773 he had sold off all his holdings, and henceforth put most of his money into mortgages on land in Scotland which, at the time of his death, amounted to some £25,000.[161] While many of his transactions over his museum and library can be traced in his account, others cannot, so that the account with Drummond's Bank does not record all his financial dealings. He had a bank account in Scotland[162] which has not yet been traced, and may have had an account with another London bank or kept considerable sums in his own hands. Between 1771 and 1779 he paid over £20,000 to a Mr. Maddison. This may well have been 'J. Maddison, Stockbroker, Charing Cross',[163] and suggests that though no dealings in stocks and shares are recorded in Hunter's bank account after 1770, he had not given up speculating. No possible explanation has yet been found for a number of other large payments made during this period.

It has been suggested that towards the end of his life Hunter overspent himself on his collections and became financially embarrassed. But his bank account shows no diminution in purchases for his Museum — and in 1781 he offered to assist the Scottish Society of Antiquaries purchase a house.[164] The idea that he was, or at least thought he was, in financial straits in part originated from G. Birkbeck Hill's edition of James Boswell's *Life of Dr. Samuel Johnson*. Recalling a visit to Johnson on the day William Hunter died, Boswell

> found him at home in the evening and had the pleasure to meet with Dr. Brocklesby . . . He mentioned a respectable gentleman, who became extremely penurious near the close of his life. Johnson said there must have been a degree of madness about him. "Not at all, Sir (said D[r] Brocklesby), his judgement was entire". Unluckily however he mentioned that although he had a fortune of £27,000, he denied himself many comforts from an apprehension that he could not afford them. "Nay, Sir, (cried Johnson) when the judgement is so disturbed that a man cannot count, that is pretty well."[165]

Commenting on this passage, Birkbeck Hill remarked that he had in his possession 'the following curious manuscript note, which is no doubt, Dr. Brocklesby's record of the conversation, [and] shews that the respectable but penurious gentleman was the famous physician, William Hunter'.[166]

> At Dr. Johnsons with J. Boswell Esq. 30 March, 1783 when Dr. Hunter dyed.
> Dr. Hunter fell a sacrifice to his last Lecture — spent £100,000 on his Collection, nothing on Himself — advised by S.J. to leave it to Glasgow where he was born and bred — proposed to have built his Anatomy of an Elephant in the Centre of his Museum which would have fixed the place unutterably.

But in L.F. Powell's revision of G. Birkbeck Hill's edition of the *Life of Dr. Johnson* it is shown, from Boswell's Journal, that the penurious gentleman was not William Hunter but Sir John Pringle.[167]

❊ ❊ ❊ ❊ ❊ ❊

Physically, Hunter was not robust and had suffered various illnesses, though he seems to have been free from the tuberculosis that affected other members of his family. As old age approached, his physical condition underwent the deterioration normal to advancing years. He had long suffered from wandering gout, rheumatism attacked his shoulders, deafness, that looked like being a problem, was mercifully only temporary. The engraving of him by J. Thornthwait shows him with spectacles, but this did not affect his hand-writing, which remained as clear and firm as in his twenties. In spite of rubbing his teeth each morning with a rough towel, one by one they fell out till, in order to speak distinctly, he had to resort to artificial teeth,[168] almost certainly made for him by Martin Van Butchell, whose wife he embalmed. [169] In spite of these infirmities, he continued to teach and collect with unabated enthusiasm till he 'fell a victim to his last lecture'.

When death was upon him, was he thinking of an escape from his failing health and from all the quarrels and disappointments of his life, or did he feel ready to depart from a well-spent life that had been full of achievement when he turned to Charles Combe and said:

> If I had strength enough to hold a pen I would write how easy and pleasant a thing it is to die(?)

William Hunter, 'the polite scholar, accomplished gentleman, the complete anatomist and probably the most perfect demonstrator as well as lecturer the world had ever seen',[170] the physician and friend of the Queen, and of many families of influence and fashion, was dead, but no preparations were made to mark his passing. Three days later, there appeared in the *Morning Chronicle* of 2 April, 1783:

> A Garrick was attended to his grave in a manner that will ever do honour to literary and theatrical characters, shall a Hunter be deposited in a silent grave privately? Forbid it Gratitude, forbid it Respect, forbid it Justice. Every lecturer in the Medical line, every physician, surgeon and apothecary, who gained their anatomical knowledge by his unwearied labours and researches must drop a tear when Dr. Hunter is no more. It is humbly recommended by the medical societies that have lost so valuable a member to meet and form a plan of public respect on so melancholy an event.

Again two days later

> The writer of last Wednesday recommends every gentleman of the Faculty in London who studied under the celebrated Dr. Hunter deposits 1 guinea at a certain Banker's, in order that his remains should be interred with every possible mark of respect. It is known to the immortal honour of this great man, that all his fortune was locked up in his grand museum, and therefore it is impossible for his executors to shew that respect which is justly due to the most celebrated anatomist of the present age. Surely it is equally just to pay every possible regard to the remains of a man who, by his important discoveries, improved to a great degree the healing art, as to make a public funeral of a theatrical character. A Chatham was a great character; a Garrick deserved fame; and a Hunter was in his professional line, equally as great as the two characters just mentioned.

Though this would seem to substantiate the idea that Hunter, at the end of his life, was financially embarrassed for ready money, his bank account does not bear this out, for at his death he was £856.11.5 in credit, and other money was on deposit in Scotland.

In spite of the efforts of the *Morning Chronicle,* either because the suggestions made met with little response or had been actively prohibited, or because the executors felt that it would have been Hunter's wish, he was buried privately at 8.00 p.m. on 5 April in the vaults of St. James's, Piccadilly, in the presence of Mr. Baillie, Dr. Pitcairn, Sir George Baker, Dr. Heberden, Mr. Cruickshank and Mr. Birnie (his draughtsman). When his friend, John Fothergill, had died two years before, 70 mourning coaches had followed his body to its resting place at Winchmore Hill. But even John was to receive only a private funeral.

The *Morning Chronicle* was not yet finished. On 8 April the writer, believing that an official stop had been put on a public funeral, and after recounting how the government had refused to grant Hunter land on which to build a public anatomy school, continued:

> Several of the Faculty were anxious to drop a tear at the grave of a Hunter: even that was refused. Are such unkind stops to excellent men who devoted their whole lives to the public good likely hereafter to promote improvement in the sciences, *etc?* The writer for particular reasons drops the subject, and would be happy, the remainder of his days to see human beings live as men and friends, at least those who render themselves useful members of Society.

The picture of William Hunter presented by Samual Foart Simmons is that of a competent scientist, but a dull man, restricted by moral rectitude from playing much part in the normal life of his day. He was, in fact, a man of vitality, fully engaged in the world about him. Quarrelsome, difficult and, at times, disagreeable, he was certainly disliked and possibly feared by some of his colleagues. Yet his achievements in science and his gift of his magnificent collections to Glasgow University demand recognition and gratitude from succeeding generations.

NOTES

1. Hunter Baillie Papers, vol. 6, f.19.
2. Hunter Baillie Papers, vol. 2, f.5.
3. Hunter Baillie Papers, vol. 1, f.51.
4. Hunter Baillie Papers, vol. 2, f.3.
5. William Cullen to William Hunter, 9 October 1751 (Thomson *loc. cit.* I, p. 541).
6. William Hunter to William Cullen, 1 August, 1751 (Thomson *loc. cit.* I, p. 541).
7. William Cullen to William Hunter, 12 July, 1751 (Thomson *loc. cit.* I p. 540).
8. Hunter Baillie Papers, vol. 2, f.5.
9. William Hunter to James Hunter, 23 March, 1745 (Houghton Library, Harvard University — Autograph Collection).
10. William Hunter, *Medical Commentaries,* Part I (London, 1762), p. 35.
11. Hunter Baillie Papers, vol. 1, f.91.
12. William Hewson's account of his dispute with William Hunter (Transcription, American Philosophical Society, Philadelphia).

> . . . Dr. Hunter having had a dispute with his brother about dividing the preparations would now insist upon having the sole property in them to avoid wrangling about a division & to avoid breaking his collection when he and I should part.

13. William Hunter's bank account. Drummond's Branch, Royal Bank of Scotland, Charing Cross, London.
14. John Hunter elected Fellow of the Royal Society, 5 February, 1767, William Hunter on 30 April, 1767.
15. Hunter Baillie Papers, vol. 2, f.10.
16. Horace Walpole, *The Yale edition of Horace Walpole's correspondence,* edited by W.S. Lewis, vols. 1-39 (Oxford, 1937-1974), vol. 32, p. 334.
17. Jesse Foot, *The Life of John Hunter* (London, 1794).
18. Royal Society of London, Library, L + P, VII, 14.
19. Willem Noortwyk, *Uteri Humani gravidi anatome et historia* (Lugduni Batavorum, 1745).
20. B.S. Albinus, *Tabulae vii uteru mulieris grandae cum iam part uriret mortuae* (Leyden 1748).
21. William Hunter, *Medical Commentaries,* Part I (London, 1762), p. 52.
22. Student notes of William Hunter's anatomy lectures, 1765. (Royal College of Physicians, Edinburgh).
23. William Hunter to Albrecht von Haller, 25 June, 1765.

> The Arteries and Veins of the Uterus grow particularly large in those branches which go to that part, which ever it be, where the Placenta is attached. Infinite numbers of both, great and small, pass into the Placenta. Infinite numbers of smaller Arteries & Veins, carrying red blood, pass likewise from the Uterus to the external Membrane of the Secundines.
> So that when the Secundines separate, in a Labour or Abortion,

the internal Surface of the Uterus bleeds by orifices of a
thousand Vessels which are necessarily torn through.

The Placenta is made up of two parts blended Intimately
together viz Uterine and Foetal. These two parts (Like the Fungi
of the Cow's Uterus and the Vessels of the Chorion) are more
easily separated in the first than in the last months of Uterogest-
ation.

The Placenta is spungy or cellular, and all its cavities filled with
the blood of the mother. The branches of all the umbilical
Vessels are bathed in that blood, like the roots of Plants in water.
The Arteries of the Uterus terminate or open directly (that is at
once, without branching into Smaller) into the cells of the
Placenta, and deposit their blood there. The Veins have the
same disposition and bring that blood again to the Uterus so
that there is a circulation through the Placenta, as through the
Corpora Cavernosa Penis. All this I know by numerous
injections and experiments.

But the Umbilical Arteries in the Placenta terminate in the
Umbilical Veins, just as in other parts of the body and injections
pass readily from the Arterial System into the Venal.

When the Arteries of the Uterus are injected the Veins are filled
as in other parts of the body; but the fluid passes always into the
whole cellular part of the Placenta, and returns from those cells
into the larger Veins of the Uterus — None passes into the
Branches of the Umbilical Vessels.

When an Umbilical Artery is injected while the Placenta
adheres to the Uterus, all the branches of both the Umbilical
Artery and of the Veins are easily filled — But none of the
injection passes into the Vessels of the Uterus — except there
happens extravasation into the Vessels of the cells of the
Placenta . . .

These *I know to be facts;* but *it is only my opinion* that the Foetus
takes supplies by an *Absorption* in the Placenta.

All those parts in the Secundines which we inject so readily by
injecting the Uterus and whose Vessels are visably continua-
tions of the Vessels of the Uterus, I say All these were originally
the efflorescence or inner membrane of the Uterus, which
separates in an abortion or birth, and comes away as much a
part of the Secundines as if it were really a part of the ovum or
contents of the Uterus. This part, and no other of the
Secundines we can inject by injecting the Uterus. It constitutes
that Membrane which covers the convex surface of the
Placenta; and by a thousand processes it dips into & is blended
with the Foetal part of the Placenta. It makes what is commonly
called the Spungy, or false, or outer Chorion. These are *facts I
am certain of.*

I call that *membrana uteri caduca,* or *Decidua* — and in London it is
commonly enough known by the name of *Hunterinana* or

Hunter's membrane. Neither young Professor Monro, nor Mr. Pott have yet laid any claim to it . . .
The state of the membranes in the first months of Pregnancy is very peculiar. The *membrana caduca,* (nostra) at the edge of the Placenta, is reflected from the Uterus to the Ovum, and continues over all the surface of the Chorion: so that it covers the Chorion in the same manner as the internal membrane of the Pericardium covers the heart . . . In the later months both Lamina of the Caduca unite, as in adhesions of the Pericardium, Pleura or Peritonaeum, and form what is called the Outer Chorion.
Experience and opportunities sooner or later will prove these observations: but a few only can be seen in any one subject.
(Burgerbibliothek, Bern. MSS. Hist. Vol. XVIII, 33).

24. Royal Society of London Library, L + P. VII.
25. *Ibid.* L + P. VII, 138.
26. John Hunter, 'On the structure of the placenta', in *Observations on Certain Parts of the Animal Economy* (London, 1786).
27. William Hunter's Scottish Will, Scottish Record Office, Edinburgh.
28. Hunter Baillie Papers belonging to the Hunterian Society at the Wellcome Library of the History of Medicine.
29. Hunter Papers, H 127.2.
30. Hunter Papers, H 127.3.
31. John Hunter on William Hewson in Lloyd G. Stevenson, 'Hewson, the Hunters and Benjamin Franklin', *J. Hist. Med.* 8 (1953), 324-328. Original in Richard Owen Papers, British Museum, Natural History.
32. William Hewson, 'Account of his quarrel with William Hunter', *loc. cit.*
33. William Hunter to Benjamin Franklin in Lloyd G. Stevenson, *loc. cit.*
34. Joseph Adams, *Memoirs of the life and doctrines of the late John Hunter, Esq.,* (London 1817).
35. William Cruickshank, 'Experiments on the Nerves . . . and on the Spinal Marrow of living Animals', *Phil. Trans.* 85 (1795), 177-189.
36. [John Douglas] 'Medical Observations and Inquiries' [a review], *Monthly Review,* 16 (1757), 541.
37. J.B. Nicholls, *Illustrations of the literary history of the eighteenth century.* (London, 1848), vol. 7, p. 260.
38. [Tobias Smollett] 'Medical Observations and Inquiries' [a review]. *Critical Review,* 4, (1757), 35.
    [J. Douglas] *A letter to the author of the Critical Review* (London 1757).
    [Tobias Smollett] 'A letter to the author of the *Critical Review*', *Critical Review,* 4 (1757), 149.
    [J. Douglas] A letter to the writer of the Critical Review, *Monthly Review,* 17 (1757), 279.
39. Hunter Papers, H57-59.
40. Hunter Papers, H254-259, 268-288, 329.
41. Hunter Papers, H292-296, 307, 309.
42. Hunter Papers, H263-265.

43. Hunter Papers, H251-252, 345-348.
44. Thomson *loc cit.* I, p. 549.
45. Hunter Baillie Papers, Royal College of Surgeons of England, vol. I, f.89.
46. Thomson *loc. cit.* I, p. 562.
47. Thomson/Cullen Papers, Box 13, Glasgow University Library.
48. Thomson *loc. cit.* I, p. 564.
49. Payments to Mr. Cullen, 1779-1780. William Hunter's bank account, *loc. cit.*
50. Thomson *loc. cit.* I, p. 562.
51. Alexander Carlyle, *Autobiography,* (Edinburgh, 1860), p. 346.
52. James Boswell, *Boswell: The ominous years 1774-1776,* edited by Charles Ryskamp and Frederick Pottle (London, 1963), p. 270.
53. 'Pam' is the knave of hearts in loo.
54. Walpole *loc. cit.* vol. 9, p. 283.
55. Walpole *loc. cit.* vol. 38, p. 78.
56. Letter from Horace Walpole to William Hunter, in J.F. Henault, *Cornélie Vestale* (Strawberry Hill, 1768), Hunterian Library, Glasgow University.
57. Sir George Macdonald, *Greek Coins in the Hunterian Collection* 3 vols. (Glasgow, 1899).
58. Lord Macaulay, quoted from George Birkbeck Hill, *Dr. Johnson, his friends and his critics* (London, 1878).
59. Hunter Baillie Papers, vol. I, f.12, f.37, f.53.
60. Walpole *loc. cit.* vol. 29, p. 86.
61. Alexander Carlyle, *Autobiography* (Edinburgh, 1860), p. 345-6.
62. Grave-robber. See Plate XII.
63. Walpole *loc. cit.* vol. 29, p. 86.
64. Walpole *loc. cit.* vol. 33, p. 241.
65. Draft of letter, William Hunter to [Professor Thomas Reid]. Hunter Baillie Papers, vol. VII, f.17a.
66. Samuel Johnson, *Letters of Samuel Johnson,* collected and edited by G. Birkbeck Hill, 2 vols. (Oxford, 1892), vol. II, pp. 261-2.
67. J.L. Clifford, *Hester Lynch Piozzi* (Mrs. Thrale), (Oxford, 1941), pp. 119-120.
68. Hester Lynch Piozzi (Mrs. Thrale), *Thraliana,* edited by K.C. Balderston, 2 vols. (Oxford, 1942), I, p. 443.
69. Letter from William Hewson to Mr. Powell, 21 August, 1770 (Transcription, American Philosophical Society Library, Philadelphia).
70. William Hunter's bank account, *loc. cit.*
71. Walpole *loc. cit.* 39, p. 35.
72. William Hunter's bank account, *loc. cit.* Cash paid to William Maynard £201.0.0.
73. The ledgers of Sir Joshua Reynolds, transcribed by Malcolm Cormack, *Walpole Society,* 42, (1970), p. 108.
74. *Correspondence of Emily, Duchess of Leinster, 1781-1814,* edited by Brian Fitzgerald, 2 volumes (1949-1953), vol. I, p. 381.
75. William Rowley, *A letter to Dr. William Hunter . . . on the dangerous tendency of medical vanity occasioned by the death of the late Lady Holland* (London, 1774).
76. Thomson *loc. cit.* I, p. 548.
77. William Rowley, *A second letter to Dr. William Hunter . . . being an answer to the illiberal criticism in the Monthly Review for November 1774* (London, 1775).

78. W. Munk, *The roll of the Royal College of Physicians,* 2nd edition, 3 vols. (London, 1878).
79. Hunter Baillie Papers, vol. I, f.13.
    M. Ancaster — Lady Ancaster, Lady-in-Waiting to the Queen.
80. Hunter Baillie Papers, vol. I, f.17.

Inverary, July 9 1776

Sir

I had the mortification of reading yesterday a Paragraph in the news papers that makes me very unhappy: it was about the King's health. Pray let me know how he does. I hope it is not true & that you will be able to give me a good account; if he is really ill sure the Queen must be Miserable & so must everybody that Knows him, tho' not all in the same degree. Pray answer this as soon as you can — I am Sir

E. Argyll Hamilton.

81. Sir George Macdonald, *Greek Coins.*
82. John Laskey, *A general account of the Hunterian Museum, Glasgow* (Glasgow, 1813), p. 71.
83. Hunter Baillie Papers, vol. I, f.82.
84. Hunter Baillie Papers, vol. I, f.53.
85. William Hunter to Robert Barclay, 20 March, 1782.
    (Royal College of Physicians and Surgeons, Glasgow).
86. Hunter Baillie Papers, vol. I, f.55.
87. Hunter Papers, H.119.
88. Hunter Baillie Papers, vol. I, f.100.
89. Thomson *loc. cit.* I, p. 554.
90. James Dennistoun, *Memoirs of Sir Robert Strange,* 2 vols. (London, 1855), vol. 2, p. 300.
91. Letter, Archibald Ingram to William Hunter, 12 June, 1764.
    Hunter Baillie Papers. Vol. VI, f.6.
    Clyde Port Authority Records, Strathclyde Region Archives.
92. William Hewson's account of his dispute with William Hunter, *loc. cit.*
93. Hunter Baillie Papers, vol. I, f.73.
94. Hunter Baillie Papers, vol. I, f.46.
95. Herbert R. Spencer, *History of British Midwifery 1650-1800* (London, 1927).
96. Hunter Baillie Papers, vol. I, f.112.
97. Hunter Baillie Papers, vol. I, f.61.
98. Hunter Baillie Papers, vol. I, f.104.
99. William Wadd, *Mems. Maxims and Memoirs* (London, 1827).
100. Walpole *loc. cit.* 35, 482.
101. Horace Walpole, *Last Journals of Horace Walpole during the reign of George III from 1771-1783,* 2 vols. (London, 1910), vol. I, pp. 205-206.
102. Advertisement at the end of James Douglas's, *Lilium Sarniense: or a description of the Guernsey-Lilly. To which is added a Botanical dissection of the Coffee berry* (London, 1725).
103. William Hunter, *Two Introductory Lectures,* (London, 1784), p. 57.
104. Douglas Figures. DF.6-40, Douglas Papers, D47.
105. Douglas Papers, D59.

106. Douglas Papers, D61.
107. Douglas Papers, D113-130.
108. Le Dran, H-F., *The operations of Surgery of Mons. Le Dran.* Translated by Thomas Gataker. With remarks, plates of the operations and a set of instruments by William Cheselden (London, 1749).
    John Douglas, *Lithotomia Douglassiana* (London, 1723).
109. Douglas Figures, DF.53-110.
    Douglas Figures, DF.86.
110. Samuel Clossy, 'The uses of anatomy', from Samuel Clossy, M.D., *The existing works,* edited with a biographical sketch by Morris H. Saffron (New York, 1967).
111. Thomas R. Forbes, 'Death of a chairman: a new William Hunter manuscript', *Yale J. Biol. Med.,* 47 (1976), 169-173.
112. Hunter Baillie Papers, vol. I, f.96.
113. William Cruickshank, 'Experiments in which . . . ova of Rabbits were found in the fallopian tubes . . .' *Phil. Trans.* 87 (1797), 197-214.
114. Karl Ernst von Baer, *De ovi mammalium et hominis genesi* (Lipsiae, 1827).
115. Ms. notes of William Cruickshank's Anatomy lectures, vol. 6. Countway Library.
116. *Ibid.* vol. I.
117. William Hunter, *A description of the human gravid uterus* (London, 1794).
118. William Cruickshank, *The anatomy of the absorbing vessels of the human body* (London, 1786).
119. John Taylor, *Records of my life,* 2 vols. (London, 1832), vol. 2, p. 262.
120. Edward Gibbon, note to William Hunter. Hunter Baillie Papers, vol. I, f.40.
    Edward Gibbon, *The memoirs of the life of Edward Gibbon,* edited by G. Birkbeck Hill (London, 1900).
121. William Robertson, author of the *History of Scotland* (1759). Principal of Edinburgh University 1762-1792.
122. Alexander Carlyle, *Autobiography* (Edinburgh, 1860), p. 346.
123. The manuscript of these lectures appeared in an auction at Sothebys, 20 February, 1978.
124. Jeremy Norman, *Twelve Manuscripts,* Catalogue Eight (Jeremy Norman & Co. Inc., San Francisco).
125. William Hunter, *Two introductory lectures delivered by Dr. William Hunter to his last class of anatomical lectures* (London, 1784).
126. Ms. notes of lectures by William Hunter. Royal College of Surgeons of England, Mss. 42.c. 28 and 29.
127. Ms. notes by William Brougham Monkhouse, later Surgeon on *H.M.S. Endeavour* on Captain Cook's first voyage, of William Hunter's lectures, c. 1755. (Wellcome Library of the History of Medicine, Ms. 2965, p. 228.)
128. Ms. notes of lectures by William Hunter. Royal College of Surgeons of England, Ms. 42.a. 31.
129. A.N. Gendrin, *Traité philosophique de médicine practique* (Paris, 1838-41).
130. Ms. notes of William Hunter's lectures on Midwifery. Countway Library, H. Ms. 6.31.
131. 'Dr. Hunter used to make this subject extremely familiar by taking a walk, as he used to call it, thro' the ear & he succeeded very well in his descriptions.' Ms. notes of W. Cruickshank's and Matthew Baillie's anatomy lectures, vol.

XIX, Francis A. Countway Library of Medicine, Boston, Mass.
132. Ms. notes of lectures on the Gravid Uterus by Wm. Hunter, M.D. & F.R.S., 1779. Countway Library, B. Ms.b.5.
133. Betsy Copping Corner, *William Shippen, Jr.* (Philadelphia, 1951).
134. William Wadd, *Mems. Maxims and Memoirs* (London, 1827).
135. Hunter Baillie Papers, vol. 1, f.31.
136. Letter from John Morgan to William Hewson. No date. College of Physicians, Philadelphia.
137. Betsy Copping Corner, *loc. cit.*
138. Anonymous, 'The Hunters and the Hamiltons', *Lancet* CCXIV (1928), 354-360, from original letters now in the Royal College of Physicians, Edinburgh.
139. Hunter Baillie Papers, vol. 1, f.77.
140. Hunter Papers, H46.
See also Kemp, *Dr. William Hunter at the Royal Academy* (Glasgow, 1975).
141. R. Knox, *Great artists and great anatomists* (London, 1852), p. 135.
142. Letter from John Burn to Benjamin Rush, Glasgow, 15 July, 1809.

Hunter's Museum has been here for some time and drawn a considerable number of students to this place. Some years ago there were not a hundred medical students in Glasgow now there are more than double that number.

(Rush Correspondence, Library Company of Philadelphia in the Pennsylvania Historical Society, Philadelphia). University Register of Professor Jeffray's (Professor of Anatomy) Medical Students, 1792-1848. Glasgow University Archives, 19039.
143. John H. Teacher, *Catalogue of the anatomical and pathological preparations of Dr. William Hunter*, 2 vols. (Glasgow, 1900).
Alice M. Marshall and J.A.G. Burton, *Catalogue of the pathological preparations of Dr. William Hunter . . . in the Museum of the Pathology Department, Glasgow Royal Infirmary* (Glasgow, 1962).
144. Matthew Baillie, *The morbid anatomy of some of the most important parts of the human body* (London, 1793).
145. Norman Moore, 'Matthew Baillie', *Dictionary of National Biography* (London, 1885).
146. Ms. William Hunter's anatomy lectures.
Royal College of Surgeons of England, Ms. 42.c. 28, p. 34.
147. Trustees' Catalogue of Minerals. Hunterian Museum Records 23. Hunterian Library, Glasgow University.
148. M.J.S. Rudwick, *The meaning of fossils* (London, 1972).
149. Trustees' Catalogue of Insects, Hunterian Museum Records 17, Hunterian Library, Glasgow University.
150. Sir Joseph Banks, Letters to Sir Charles Blagden, Revesby Abbey, 20 September and 1 November, 1782. Royal Society of London Library, Banks and Blagden Correspondence (B10 & 95).
151. F.W. Hope, 'The autobiography of John Christian Fabricius', translated from the Danish. *Trans. Ent. Soc. Lond.* 4 (1845), I-XVI.
152. R.A. Staig, *The Fabrician types of insects in the Hunterian Collection at Glasgow*

University, Parts 1 and 2 (Cambridge, 1931 & 1940).

153. Peter Dance, *Shell Collecting* (London, 1966), p. 110.

154. John Laskey, *A general account of the Hunterian Museum, Glasgow* (Glasgow 1813).

155. Letters of Professor Lockhart Muirhead to his wife while he was packing up the Hunterian Museum in London for its removal to Glasgow, 1807. Glasgow University Library, Ms. Gen. 1354, 25-65.

156. *The Hunterian Collection,* Iveagh Bequest, Kenwood. With introduction by A. McLaren Young (London County Council, 1952).

157. Tobias Smollett, Letter to William Hunter, 11 August, 1763. M. Knapp, *The letters of Tobias Smollett,* (Oxford, 1970). From the original in the Hyde Collection, Somerville, New Jersey.

158. Hunter Papers, H227-246.

159. Hunterian Ms. 315.

160. William Hewson's account of his dispute with William Hunter, *loc. cit.*

161. Account of charge and discharge of Dr. William Hunter's estate. Hunter Baillie Papers, vol. 6. f.37.

162. James Baillie to William Hunter, 15 November 1775. Hunter Baillie Papers, vol. 1. f.5.

163. Henry Kent, *Kent's Directory for the year 1794* (London, 1794).

164. The Earl of Buchan to Mr. James Cumyng, 3 March, 1781.

> Sir,
>
> I have the pleasure to inform you that my efforts with relation to the Society of Scotch Antiquarians have been accompanied with so much sucess & there seems now so little likelihood of being disappointed in the attainment of the Fund necessary for our modest views, that I desire you will further the purchase of Coll: Campbell's House which if the purchase money is not required to be paid up fully till Whitsun day 1782, I can freely venture to purchase the House in Trust for the Society, and take my chance of my own support from the public. Dʳ· William Hunter has come forward to further the views of the Society in the most friendly manner & has signified to me that he will give freely and largely to the funds of the Society, as soon as he shall see from the other subscriptions what will be required to enable us to prosecute our designs.
>
> I suppose 850 or 900 £ at most will be accepted by Coll: Campbell. . .
>
> Buchan.

(Archives of the Society of Antiquaries of Scotland, National Museum of Antiquities, Edinburgh.)

165. James Boswell, *Life of Dr. Samuel Johnson,* edited by George Birkbeck Hill (Oxford, 1887), vol. VI, p. 176.

166. Samuel Johnson, *Letters of Samuel Johnson,* collected and edited by G. Birkbeck Hill, 2 vols. (Oxford, 1892), II, p. 437.

167. James Boswell, *Life of Johnson,* edited by George Birkbeck Hill. Revised and enlarged by L.F. Powell, 6 vols. (Oxford, 1934-1950), vol. 4, p. 510.

Dr. Brocklesby came . . . and we had much conversation about Sir John Pringle . . . He mentioned his sad failing and narrowness in the latter part of his life . . . Dr. Johnson said there must have been a degree of madness about him. Dr. Brocklesby said his Judgement was entire. But when he mentioned his being worth £27,000 yet unwilling to keep a carriage because he feared he would die of Want, "Nay Sir" said Dr. Johnson. . .

(Boswell Papers, XV. 188).

In Dr. Brocklesby's account of this meeting, no mention is made of the conversation about Sir John Pringle, and since Brocklesby's remark 'Dr. Hunter — spent £100,000 on his museum, nothing on himself', appeared to relate to the 'penurious gentleman', therefore Hill assumed it was Dr. Hunter.

168. Ms. notes of William Cruickshank's lectures, XX volumes. Countway Library.
169. Payments to Van Butchell, who was a maker of false teeth, of £42.0.0. in 1772 and £31.10 in 1776 (William Hunter's bank account, Drummond's Branch, Royal Bank of Scotland), may well have been for false teeth. Made from walrus tusk ivory, they decayed and had to be replaced periodically.
170. Joseph Adams, *Memoirs of the life and doctrines of the late John Hunter, Esq.,* (London, 1817).